The Integrity Manual
For Leaders In A Global Society

Gwen Smith Brown

Soul Source Press, Inc.

Maryland ▲ USA

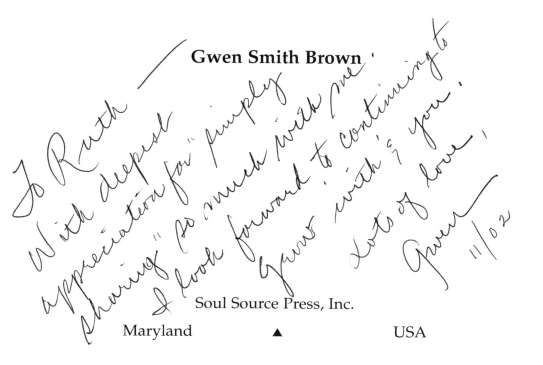

To Ruth
With deepest
appreciation for simply
sharing so much with me
I look forward to continuing to
grow with you.
Lots of love,
Gwen
11/02

THE INTEGRITY MANUAL FOR LEADERS IN A GLOBAL SOCIETY

Published by
SOUL SOURCE PRESS, INC.
P.O. BOX 590
TEMPLE HILLS, MD 20748-0590 U.S.A.

Library of Congress Card Number: 00-190303
Brown, Gwen Smith
The Integrity Manual for Leaders in a Global Society

Includes Index
ISBN 0-9700008-0-4

First Edition
Printed in the United States of America

Cover design by Rick Clark, Rick Clark Illustration & Design

Peace cannot be maintained by force. It can only be achieved by understanding.

—Author Unknown

The world public has become disenchanted with both the political and financial leadership, which it no longer trusts to solve the problems of historical crises. Further more, all the individuals of humanity are looking for the answer to what the little individual can do that can't be done by great nations and great enterprises.

—R. Buckminster Fuller

DEDICATION PAGE

This book is dedicated to my mother,
Alice Frederick Smith. *She provided encouragement, support and motivation during the writing of this book and Integrity Manuals to follow. She believed in their value to society. Through her own life of critical analysis and quiet activism, she taught me to analyze with my heart and to resist wrong.*

I miss you, Mom.

ACKNOWLEDGMENTS

Thanks is the most wonderful, and at the same time, the most under used word in any language. To each of those listed below and others whose names I may have inadvertently omitted, I express deep appreciation.

Carolyn Myss, author of *Energy Anatomy*, Gary Zukav, author of *The Seat of the Soul* and Neale Donald Walsh, author of *Conversations With God, Book 1*, prepared me for this work and inspired me to embrace it. I thank you for those gifts gained through your writings.

Many people, before Dr. Helen Stewart, predicted aspects of my future work — the work I do today. But Helen gave me minute details and told me I was to write this book. A very powerful physical intuitive, Helen continues to be a strong supporter, counselor and sister-friend. I owe her the greatest debt of all. Helen Billings helped me "see" myself in this role and to know I had work to do. Her loving support through tough times will always be remembered. Sophia Dickerson has shown the way and believed in this work from the very beginning. I am indebted to you still. The people of Vieques, Puerto Rico helped me to embrace the work of writing; the staff at the Fajardo Inn, Fajardo, Puerto Rico saw success for me and wanted to be sure they knew when I was going to be on Oprah. Gracias! You helped me keep the faith. To Carlos Alberto Zayas I was a complete stranger, but he spent hours working on my laptop in his home so I could keep on writing. I will never forget you, Carlos.

The technicians behind the scenes are the reason the show goes on at all. To my editor, Mary Ellen Butler, I owe the deepest gratitude for thoughtful, caring attention to this work. Your touch and your counsel have made the book an "easy read." I look forward to working with you again. Elvis Lewis at KCR Digital Printing and Imaging, Inc. got into my head and understood what this work was about and translated that to his team. He also made the technical aspects of production something even I could understand. I owe the cover design and the rendition of the tools to the remarkable artistic genius of Rick Clark. Thanks to Rachel Phillips for layout assistance. Richard Warr gets my deep appreciation for his graphic support in the early days of this project and for final layout and design. To all of you, my deepest gratitude for your help and support.

Several organizations and groups have been important to this work. Through rigorous training, Simba, Inc., re-defined integrity for me and forced me to be more attentive to every word I spoke. Thank you, Sterling "White Buffalo Woman" and Wild Woman International for providing a space and place for me to gain more clarity and focus and a chance to know who I really am. The Artist's Way group at First Church of Religious Science in Oakland, CA and the Reverend Annie Green, facilitator extraordinaire, helped me learn to play again and build my writing around my playing. The memory of their warm encouragement continues to be a source of support.

I thank God for friends all over the country who have held me and this work in their hearts. I especially thank God for the life of Lillie Earls and Dr. William L. Spivey for their roles in my survival so I could do this work; for Dr. Claire Nelson, who "hooked me up" with many of the team members necessary to bring a project like one's first book to fruition; for Ouida J. Cooper-Rodriguez, who knew I was ready even when I had trouble knowing it; for Gail Elleby, who needed to know how the book was coming at least once a week and who *asked* to be a reader of the manuscript and made sure I moved forward by providing advice, comments, and loving encouragement when things bogged down; for my buddy, Dr. Woody Carter, who gets my thanks for supporting me lovingly through tough times and for believing in this work because I'm me; for believing in this work because I'm me; for the consummate sister-friend, Velva Spriggs, who is truly always there when I need her and was there when quitting felt like the best option; for Patricia Hope, who provides loving counsel, keen insight and sharp analysis; for Helen Davis, my spiritual sister, who graciously supported me and this work in every way; and for the many people who have been advisory to me throughout this whole process.

My deep appreciation to literary agent, Denise Stinson, who threw down the gauntlet which landed at my feet, quivering, and stopped me in my tracks for six months when she asked, "Who are you that anyone would want to read what *you* write about integrity?" And to Maggie Bedrosian and Lynne Waymon, directors of the 4th Washington Writers Workshop, and fellow participants, especially Wendy Kinney and Thalia Doukas, who helped me find the answer to that question, I am extremely grateful. I thank you all for your vision, your creativity and your generous, wise and wonderful counsel. To members and ministers of Takoma Park Metaphysical Chapel (Silver Spring, MD), especially Senior Minister Jim Webb, for being able to "see" for me when I couldn't and for lovingly pushing me forward. To the librarians of the Prince George's County Memorial Library System, especially those at the Hillcrest Heights and Oxon Hill Branches, and to those at the Library of Congress and the Martin Luther King, Jr. Central Library in Washington, DC, I appreciate your guidance and assistance with the research necessary to ground this book and those to follow. To Paul Coates, of Black Classic Press (Baltimore, MD), I express deep appreciation for your gentle, but right-on-the-mark education on the complexities of the publishing industry and the nudge that got me to print this volume ... now!

Deepest gratitude to my family. You have been extremely supportive and helpful, especially my brother, Gary, without whom this book could not have been written, and my Mom, who saw great importance to this work and pushed me to get it done fast! My thanks to my daughter, Diarra, my pearl, who supports me in everything, listens with interest to every progress report and joyfully provides her well-honed marketing and website design skills.

Most of all, I thank Spirit for entrusting this work to me and for providing all the necessary resources–including all of those mentioned above, those inadvertently omitted and those yet to come.

To all of my well-wishers, I acknowledge you for sending wonderfully positive energy into the Universe for me. *Keep it flowing! My love, peace and blessings to you all!*

Gwen Smith Brown
March 2000

CONTENTS

ACKNOWLEDGMENTS v

FOREWORD by Daniel Schorr xiii

INTRODUCTION xvii

    Why a Book on Integrity in Leadership Now? xvii
    Road Map to Integrity xx
    How to Use This Book xxii

SECTION I: THE STRUGGLE FOR INTEGRITY IN OUR LIVES

CHAPTER 1: INTEGRITY 3
    What It Is 3
    How to Know It 5
    How to Practice It 6
    The Tools 6
    Related Concepts 11
    Our Definition 13

CHAPTER 2: PERSONAL INTEGRITY 14
    Key to Achieving Integrity in All of Life 14
    Integrity With the Self 16
    ISSUES:
        Owning Your Own Power 19
        Living Your Life Purpose 20
    Integrity With Oneself 22
    ISSUES:
        Speaking One's Mind 22
        Racism, Sexism and Other Prejudice 22

CHAPTER 3: INTEGRITY IN LEADERSHIP— CIVIL SERVANTS 24
    ISSUES:
        Sexual Harassment 24
        Taking Advantage of the Employer 25
        Playing Favorites in Funding 26
        De-emphasizing the Truth 26
        Whistle Blowing 27
        Promotions and Awards 28

CHAPTER 4: INTEGRITY IN LEADERSHIP—
ELECTED and APPOINTED OFFICIALS 29

ISSUES:

Animosity Between Branches Of
Government 30

Unbridled Partisanship and
Use of Smoke Screens 32

Selling the Vote 34

Wasting Money/Pork Barrels 34

Lopsided Treaties & Trade Agreements 37

Misuse Of and Disrespect For International
Organizations 38

Responsibility to the People 40

CHAPTER 5: INTEGRITY IN LEADERSHIP—
MILITARY OFFICIALS 42

ISSUES:

Development, Testing and Use of Chemical
& Biological Weapons 43

Testing Of Chemical & Biological Weapons
On Our Own Personnel 44

Use of Land Mines 45

Over-Zealous Disciplinary Action, Harassment
and Scapegoating 46

**SECTION II: ACHIEVING INTEGRITY
WITH PRACTICE**

How to Use This Section 49

Practicing Integrity Form 50

CHAPTER 6: OWNING YOUR OWN POWER 51

CHAPTER 7: LIVING YOUR LIFE PURPOSE 53

CHAPTER 8: SPEAKING ONE'S MIND 55

CHAPTER 9: RACISM, SEXISM and
OTHER PREJUDICE 58

CHAPTER 10: SEXUAL HARASSMENT 61

CHAPTER 11: TAKING ADVANTAGE OF
THE EMPLOYER 64

CHAPTER 12: PLAYING FAVORITES IN FUNDING 67

CHAPTER 13: DE-EMPHASIZING THE TRUTH 70

CHAPTER 14: WHISTLE BLOWING 73

CHAPTER 15: PROMOTIONS AND AWARDS 77

CHAPTER 16: ANIMOSITY BETWEEN BRANCHES
OF GOVERNMENT 80

CHAPTER 17: UNBRIDLED PARTISANSHIP and
USE OF SMOKE SCREENS 84

CHAPTER 18: SELLING THE VOTE 87

CHAPTER 19: WASTING MONEY/PORK BARRELS 90

CHAPTER 20: LOPSIDED TREATIES AND TRADE
AGREEMENTS 93

CHAPTER 21: MISUSE OF and DISRESPECT FOR
INTERNATIONAL ORGANIZATIONS 96

CHAPTER 22: RESPONSIBILITY TO THE PEOPLE 99

CHAPTER 23: DEVELOPMENT, TESTING AND
USE OF CHEMICAL & BIOLOGICAL
WEAPONS 102

CHAPTER 24: TESTING OF CHEMICAL & BIOLOGICAL
WEAPONS ON OUR OWN
PERSONNEL 104

CHAPTER 25: USE OF LAND MINES 106

CHAPTER 26: OVER-ZEALOUS DISCIPLINARY ACTION,
HARASSMENT and SCAPEGOATING 109

SECTION III: MEASURING CHANGE IN INTEGRITY LEVELS

CHAPTER 27: USING THE INTEGRITY QUOTIENT
TO MEASURE OUR INTEGRITY
LEVEL 113

CHAPTER 28: USING THE INTEGRITY QUOTIENT
TO MEASURE INTEGRITY LEVELS
OF POLITICAL LEADERS 116

AFTERWORD 119

NOTES 123

INDEX 131

FOREWORD[1]

Arthur Schlesinger is authority for the fact that no Kennedy speech went through as much redrafting as his inaugural address. And no sentence was more worked-on than, "Ask not what your country can do for you. . . ." The theme had appeared in campaign speeches around the country in such forms as, "We do not campaign stressing what our country is going to do for us." The extra work on that line paid off in an inspiring call to service beyond self that can still draw us here a generation later.

President Kennedy and I were of the same generation. In fact, he was nine months younger than myself. Our generation had known national service in World War II. At a time of confrontation with the Soviet Union a summons to serve the nation had a familiar ring. His speech dwelt more with global dangers than domestic traumas. But, lest he be accused of neglecting problems at home, he added, in his commitment to human rights, the words, ". . . . at home and around the world."

At home, it seemed natural that our national government should guide and mobilize our energies. This was the era of the Peace Corps and its domestic counterpart, VISTA. The era of the Johnsonian Great Society whose roots President Kennedy had planted. The era when teachers, doctors, lawyers, were enlisted by government to serve those in need of their services. Over the heads of state and local government, the Federal government reached out to stimulate community action in the ghetto and it gave support to the activists, the preachers, and students who were making the civil rights revolution.

But then the Great Society and the idea of looking to government for leadership foundered on the Vietnam War and its offspring, Watergate. Grizzled veterans of Watergate will remember that symbol of disillusionment, Gordon Strachan. The 27-year-old Haldeman assistant had been caught up in the White House conspiracy. Before the Senate Watergate committee, live on television, he testified about how he had been led astray. And when Senator Joe Montoya of New Mexico asked him what he would advise other young men planning careers in Washington, he said, "My advice would be to stay away."

Strachan is now a lawyer in Park City, Utah, and a board member of the Salt Lake City Olympic Organizing Committee. In preparing this speech, it occurred to me to ask him whether he is still turned off by government service. He did not return my call.

Among those disturbed by the "stay away" mentality was Mortimer Caplin, President Kennedy's IRS Commissioner and himself an exemplary public servant. In a speech in 1975, Caplin said not all of Strachan's generation were "as easily beguiled by power as he was." Mortimer quoted Edmund Burke's observation, "The only thing necessary for the triumph of evil is for good men to do nothing." And he asked, "What would the state of our nation be if the able and good withdrew?"

Alas, we are on the way to finding out. The Reagan-Bush Iran-Contra scandal followed the Nixon scandal and was, in turn, followed by the Clinton impeachment scandal. One effect of the scandals has been oppressive disclosure requirements for job candidates and inquisitions into their past histories that drive many away. Alienation from government has become a cliché, a settled fact, many convinced that government is more a problem than a solution.

What does it mean that, for the second successive year, the armed forces, although offering lavish sign-up bonuses, have been unable to reach their recruiting goals? What does it mean that voter turnout in national elections keeps declining? What does it mean that a recent Wilson Center study found Americans of mixed minds about government, wanting its services but suspicious of its power?

Does this mean that President Kennedy's summons to serve the country would fall on deaf ears today? One does not hear many ringing calls to public service from today's crop of Presidential candidates. That maverick, Senator John McCain, stands out for his pledge to renew faith in government "so that Americans can believe once again that public service is a summons to duty and not a lifetime of privilege."

I have no doubt that altruism and compassion (without the "conservative" modifier) runs through our nation like an underground stream. It is most evident at a time of earthquake or flood disaster. It can be seen in the way a child fallen into a well becomes a matter of national concern. Or the national shock over a school or church shooting. That Wilson Center study that found Americans so ambivalent about government said that 54 per cent of detractors of government still favor increased aid for low-income families.

But the fact is that, while Americans on the whole do not lack altruism and a bent for public service, today public service has been redefined by many as service not necessarily through the government, but to the community.

May I mention my son, Jonathan, and my daughter, Lisa, who answered President Kennedy's summons their own ways? Jonathan, on graduation from Yale, joined the first contingent of Teach for America volunteers and spent three years teaching hard-to-teach kids in an urban high school in Pasadena. Lisa, on graduating from Harvard, joined the service group City Year, which became the model for AmeriCorps. Then she went to Harvard Business School for an MBA because she believed that non-profits needed skilled managers. Now she is the director of business enterprise for the Pine Street Inn, New England's biggest homeless shelter.

Jonathan and Lisa are not unique (except to their parents). There are many ways to serve the community. Former Treasury Secretary Robert Rubin did by becoming chairman of the Local Initiatives Support Group, which aids community development corporations. Some may pass up more profitable opportunities to become teachers or social workers. Some others may donate organs of their bodies. Still others may donate money, like Bill Gates and Ted Turner. (Twenty years ago Turner told me that how much money you amass is how you keep score. More recently he has decided that how much you give away is how you really keep score.)

On campuses nationwide, volunteers join to help people in the transition from welfare by making them ready for employment, coaching them for drivers' tests, finding bargain-price clothing, picking convenient bus routes.

It would be nice to be able to conclude that what you can do for your country can be done in your community, ignoring a largely discredited government. And many in government would be happy to abdicate responsibility by shifting the burden to "a thousand points of light:" to churches, philanthropies, and other non-governmental efforts.

But it cannot work without government. Bill Shore, who founded Share Our Strength, an effective hunger relief and anti-poverty organization that has mobilized sources of private wealth to support more than 450 community-based service organizations, has written of the limitations of private effort when performed in isolation. "Reforming and revitalizing our political institutions to make them more responsive and more effective is as important and as worthwhile as ever," he says.

Inspiring examples of communal effort will not go very far unless underpinned by an enlightened national policy, national leadership, and, yes, national money.

John Gardner says that government "will not become worthy of trust until citizens take positive action to hold it to account."

Once, when Kennedy was President, we could ask the government to lead the people. Today we must ask the people to lead the government. Public service may begin at home. But it cannot end there.

Daniel Schorr, Senior Analyst
National Public Radio
Washington, D. C.

INTRODUCTION

WHY A BOOK ON INTEGRITY IN LEADERSHIP NOW?

According to an opinion survey conducted for Booker's Bourbon Whiskey in 1998,[2] 33% of adults in the United States of America say the most important thing they learned from their father is to "Always tell the truth." That finding is more remarkable for what it does *not* say than what it *does* say. It raises questions, such as: "Did the other 67% not learn that at all?" "Did other fathers teach something different about telling the truth?" "What did mothers teach about telling the truth?" Let's assume the worst: that the other 67% did not learn this lesson at all. That would help explain the crisis of integrity gripping the United States of America today, from elected officials at the highest reaches of government to children in grade school.

If you are reading this book, you have a reason for being interested in the subject of integrity. Have you been wronged, damaged or hurt by someone or some entity whose actions you feel lacked integrity? Are you troubled by an act of your own which lacked integrity? Has a loved one been left broken and resentful by an injustice of another? Are you wondering how to instill integrity in your children? Are you concerned about the future of your country or the world given the lack of integrity which abounds? Whatever your interest, you are not alone. I am constantly told by people just like you how much this work is needed because of all of those concerns cited above.

The integrity crisis is of international proportions. The evidence is indisputable. For example:

- Many western nations are outraged at North Korea's development and testing of nuclear weapons capability and worst, it's purported sale of that technology to India and Pakistan. Why? Western nations have been testing nuclear weapons and selling the technology to other European powers for decades. Similarly, they have been selling huge quantities of "weapons of mass destruction" to other countries creating an enormous economic boon for themselves. If it is good for one, why not for all?

- Throughout much of the world, people are outraged at Iraqi President Saddam Hussein's repeated breaking of "promises" related to divestment of Iraq's weapons of mass destruction. However, there was little discussion among the populace in the United States of America, or by its media, of the impact on the United Nations' monitoring mission and its world credibility caused by the spying done by that country's representatives to the monitoring team.

- Several years ago, a new embassy built in Russia for the United States of America was found to be uninhabitable after it was discovered that listening devices had been built into and throughout the structure.

- Ethnic cleansing, the act of removal by death, torture and forced relocation from certain geographic areas of people of a certain ethnic background, is occurring or has occurred in Yugoslavia, Turkey, Afghanistan, Rwanda and Sudan. Other nations provided the arms and trained the armies of the leaders who carry out such atrocities. In the cases of Yugoslavia and Turkey, other countries provide tremendous amounts of weaponry knowing the leaders' disdain for and acts against specific members of their populations. Where is the integrity in such arms sales? Are the providers of arms less to blame for the carnage?

- There was much outrage and consternation about whether or not President William Jefferson (Bill) Clinton (United States of America) lied under oath in a sexual harassment case. He admitted that he had an improper sexual relationship with a White House intern and that he did attempt to cover it up. Early in 1999, President Clinton was impeached by the United States of America's House of Representatives. The vote in the United States Senate fell short of the number required to convict the President of lying under oath about that illicit relationship. Many people are still upset and disheartened by the whole affair. Does the requirement for integrity and modeling character not exist at such high levels in our government? Was the Congress acting with integrity when it released the sordid details electronically world-wide? Where is the line?

- In March 1999, the most recent of many trials stemming from the 1980's AIDS scandal that rocked France ended. Former Prime Minister Laurent Fabius and former Social Affairs Minister Georgina Dufoix were acquitted of manslaughter charges; Ms. Dufoix' health minister, Edmond Herve, was convicted of manslaughter in the cases of two of the seven victims who brought this suit. (Several of the participants in the suit have died since filing suit.) Notwithstanding the conviction, in an unprecedented action, he was given no sentence. The suits stem from French health agencies' use of untested blood at a time when human immunodeficiency virus (HIV) contamination was believed to cause Acquired Immune Deficiency Syndrome or AIDS.[3] Over 4000 persons received the untested blood. Hundreds if those transfused have died of AIDS related causes. Such incidents betray our trust in government and can produce in us cynicism and hopelessness.

Those are some of the obvious examples that march across our newspaper and television news headlines every day. There are new stories daily. Why? Because although integrity is more than honesty, it starts with simple honesty. Nobody is discussing the fact that lying is a national pastime— in the United States of America, at least. People lie and cheat on their taxes. Spouses cheat on each other at the rate of 60% for women and 65% for men.[4] Students buy term papers from others and steal exams at a growing rate. The same Congress in the United States of America, that soothes public concern one year by creating new programs to help those most in need quietly cuts funding the next year, ensuring those programs' failure. This is a form of lying to the public. It is misuse of the public trust.

The integrity crisis is global and is evident in all levels of civil society world-wide. If we are to experience the magnificent possibilities of the new millennium, we must go forward into the 21st century embracing the *practice of integrity.*[5] Throughout the 20th century, leaders around the world have been spitting bullets at each other out of anger, fear and frustration. I challenge the leaders of the world to move *beyond* spitting bullets. You must. Not only because you are caught in a no-win cycle, but our children are imitating you. They too are spitting bullets out of anger, fear and pain — in Colorado, Oregon, Georgia, to name a few of the states in the United States of America that have experienced mass school shootings. Around the world thousands of children are involved in making war. And why not? Millions of them are angry, frightened and in pain over the suffering, loss of homes and loss of adult caretakers.

To have integrity among government workers, elected, appointed and military officials and others we consider our leaders, we must have integrity ourselves — as individuals. It all starts with you and me. In our daily lives as individuals – as parents, children, employees, employers, producers of goods and services, non-profit managers, church members, clergy and government workers – we face numerous opportunities to practice integrity. In this book, I talk about how each of us can live life more fully through the practice of integrity as we confront those challenges. I believe the majority of the world public does do the right thing most of the time. I know we agonize over some of the decisions we have to make. I am not suggesting that we are all totally devoid of character. I acknowledge and salute you for doing the right thing most of the time. I am saying, however, that we must take it to a higher level and take the high road even more than we usually do because when we are *really* practicing integrity, we will not tolerate others, including leaders, who do less. While we look to political leaders, professional athletes, famous entertainers, and other highly visible people to be role models for our children, we overlook the most important models in our children's lives: first, the caring adults who raise them and next, the people they live among. The answer to the question, "What should I tell my child?" about the behavior of public figures is much less important than what we are saying to them, in words *and* actions, that reflect our own dishonesty or excuse theirs and similar behavior they see around them daily.

ROAD MAP TO INTEGRITY

Some people think right action is old fashioned, that nobody else is doing it and that it's not the way to get ahead. We look at some of our most successful corporate magnates and feel they could not possibly have gotten "all that money" honestly. True, some of them didn't. But others did. Many of us believe we can cheat our way to abundance more easily than we can work and will our way there.

But because wrong-doing produces guilt and anxiety, more of us will be happier and healthier if we move forward to right-doing. It is consistent and in harmony with our essence or nature. I wrote this book as a guide to all of us for moving forward to lives marked by integrity in a way that is also easy for us to achieve. I believe most of us are willing to work to improve our character in the same way we work to build strong muscles and a healthy heart. But we don't know how to develop integrity in our children and ourselves or we think it's too hard or too late. It is not too hard and it is definitely not too late.

Evolving, through the practice of integrity, is the global imperative for the 21st century. If you will let it, this book can be the starting point for conversations about integrity, what you want from your leaders, indeed what you are demanding from them and holding them accountable for *and* it can truly become your road map to the **practice of integrity** in your personal life and by those in political life and other walks of life as well.

Like the rest of us, government workers as well as those in political and military positions need help in figuring out which options represent the choice of integrity. This is especially true in our increasingly complex world. In some cases, we recognize the choice of integrity but rationalize that "in this one instance" we need to choose a different (and less honorable) course. We may even rationalize this choice as the honorable thing to do. A friend said to me, when she read a part of this book, that "You make integrity sound like it's black or white." Integrity **is** black or white. Rationalizers are trying to find the gray!

I also wrote this book to contribute to and promote an international conversation about integrity and a world-wide support system for integrity. We need to make it okay to explore with others, on either side of the aisle, regardless of political labels or color and style of the uniforms, across national borders and the oceans which physically separate us, our indecision or concern about a particular choice. We need to support each other in our individual efforts to practice integrity. We need to remind others to look for and take the course of integrity. All this because integrity is a *global* imperative.

Finally, I wrote this book on integrity in leadership because there are tools I want to share with you which work even when struggling to unravel complex political issues. These tools

(a) help me recognize the right thing to do; and

(b) help me do the right thing in a way that is comfortable for me.

The practice of integrity is much less difficult if you allow yourself the comfort of picking the easiest way to do the right thing in each situation. Most people don't stop to think about the options they have or can generate for how they can do the right thing. Practicing integrity is a two-part process and if you go through the two parts one-at-a-time, you will find practicing integrity easier and maybe more fun than you thought. You first have to recognize the right thing to do and secondly, find the easiest way to do it.

HOW TO USE THIS BOOK

This book consists of three sections. Here is how they are organized.

Section I, The Struggle for Integrity in Our Lives, consists of five chapters. The first chapter explores and defines my concept of integrity. As you will see, it is a different concept from the standard dictionary definition. I also explain how to use the 7-Step Process for Practicing Integrity. The second chapter uses real life examples of what I call personal "integrity challenges" that many of us encounter every day. Chapters three through five illustrate how public figures in particular, including civil servants, elected officials, appointed officials and military officials, face such "integrity challenges" and how they, as leaders can practice the 7-Step Process to make decisions that help create a better world.

Although chapters three through five — highlight integrity challenges faced by a specific group of public servants, they are meant for all of us to read. We need to understand how the 7-Step Process can be used by our leaders because I want us to monitor our public figures. If they are not practicing the 7-Step Process, we need to urge them to do so because that is what will earn them our continued support.

Section II, Achieving Integrity With Practice, takes a closer look at each of the specific integrity challenges introduced in Chapters two through five of Section I. Chapters 6 through 26 of Section II include exercises with examples for strengthening our practice of integrity. In order to get the most out of Section II, you should read Section I first. Thereafter, however, the reader may pick and choose the issues from Section II to concentrate on for further personal study and growth.

Section III, Measuring Change in Integrity Levels, consists of Chapters 27 and 28, the final chapter of the book. Chapter 27, Using The Integrity Quotient (TIQ) to Measure Our Integrity Level, introduces a method for calculating our own present and future integrity levels. Chapter 28, Using The Integrity Quotient to Measure Integrity Levels of Political Leaders, shows how to use The Integrity Quotient as a process for monitoring the integrity levels of public figures. I hope that we as citizens will use this method to encourage higher standards of integrity among our leaders in civil service, elected, appointed and military positions. Governing is a privilege; discharging the responsibility with integrity is critically important to creating the environment for global progress. Integrity *is* an imperative for the 21st century.

This book should be read slowly, allowing time for reflection and self assessment. It may be used as a textbook, handbook, guide or desk reference for everyday situations. It can be the focus of staff and other group discussions. I hope I have provided you a format that is pleasing, a message which is easily understood and a process you will enjoy using. The *work* of practicing integrity is now OURS to do. Let's get going!

SECTION I

THE STRUGGLE FOR INTEGRITY IN OUR LIVES

CHAPTER 1:
Integrity

INTEGRITY: WHAT IT IS

It is possible to use the words "politician" and "integrity" in the same sentence without feeling dubious, or even laughing. We only have to decide that's what we want — public servants with integrity. But, what exactly do we mean when we say "integrity?"

INTEGRITY comes from the Latin "in" + "teg" meaning "untouched, hence undivided, whole." Two meanings are listed. The first:

> *Soundness of and adherence to moral principle and character; uprightness, honesty.*

The second:

> *The state of being whole, entire, or undiminished.*[6]

While the dictionary treats these as separate definitions, I believe they are very much connected. One cannot be whole and undiminished *unless and until* one is **practicing** adherence to moral principle and character. In this work, I further differentiate integrity from a "state of being," as cited in the second definition above and offer instead that it is a ***practice*** ... a *way* of being.

Honesty, adherence to moral principle and uprightness may not be easy to practice all the time in all situations. In that regard, integrity is like balance. Achieving balance in one's life is a day-to-day effort — whether it is balance in our diet, exercise, relaxation or leisure. Integrity, like balance, has to be practiced every day. Integrity can no longer be a philosophy or policy for the other person to live by or for certain persons to be judged by. Integrity cannot be reserved for certain relationships. To be a **people** with integrity, a **nation** with integrity in the world community, we **each** have to practice integrity — each day, one situation at a time.

To be a world with integrity, each nation must practice, one situation at a time, all the time. We live in a global society; seconds separate us from the farthest point on the Earth. The oneness of life is better understood today— at the dawn of the 21st century. Destruction of the forests in South America causes the global warming that affects animal, plant and human life, changes the world's weather and increases the rate of growth of disease and illness. To protect life as we know it, we have to become a global society with integrity.

The *practice of integrity* is a dynamic two-fold process. It is the act of (a) thoughtfully considering every decision for its likelihood to produce or foster wholeness, alignment with one's center, or universal good; then (b) identifying options, choosing and then exercising the option that does produce the greatest good or unity. To *practice integrity* forces the practice of honesty. We cannot assess a situation and decide on an action only because our own interests are served. We live in a complex social structure with many overlapping relationships. Each life impacts other lives around it. If we practice integrity, we will not be able to make a totally self-serving choice for action if we go through the process described below.

Practicing integrity is an individualized process. The first part in the process is knowing the right thing to do (or not do). Identifying the right thing to do may not be easy because of the circumstances under which one has to make a choice. Let's take, for example, a mother who is having a hard time feeding her children and sees them crying every day because they are hungry. The first part in the process (what is right) suggests the question, "Should the woman feed her children?" Let's assume we believe the answer to be "Yes." Once we know *what* we should do, the question becomes *how* to do it. That is the second part of the process. It may be easier for the mother in our example to rationalize stealing food rather than looking for other options and taking the high road. Likewise, some readers of this book may disagree that stealing food for her children constitutes a break with integrity for the desperate mother. I maintain that it does.

Deciding **how** to do the right thing is the second part of practicing integrity. How to get food without stealing it might take courage or cause deep anxiety. On the other hand, it could be a very freeing experience. To go to social service organizations or a soup kitchen is seen as degrading by some. To others, asking a relative or a parent who scorned us for the decisions we made means groveling. Still others find asking a grocer for fruits and vegetables demeaning. One mother, facing these choices, may choose to ask the grocer for food. Another may seek the help of a family member. A third may take her children to a daily meal service program. This is where individual choice comes in. Each gets to choose the option for doing right which feels most comfortable.

To *practice integrity* requires that we keep looking for solutions that bring about the greatest good, wholeness or unity with one's center or the Self. The dynamic process does not end with the first solution we choose. We must be open to the revelation of more and better solutions to the same issue in the future.

INTEGRITY: HOW TO KNOW IT

Let's look at a family dealing with the issue of a teenaged child who is using alcohol. The **parents** are clear about the rightness/wrongness of alcohol use by their child; it is wrong. The parents are clear about their parental role: "This is behavior we do not condone; we will respond to this behavior." They agree they will confront the child. But that is where they become stumped. What else will they do? They feel that to confront the child but leave everything else the same invites continuation of the same behavior. What is the appropriate intervention? The appropriate intervention is the one which brings the parents peace, inner peace. You will know when you have made the right choice for you in practicing integrity when you *feel* a sense of peace. For one parent, that might look like sending the child out of town to remove him/her from his/her environment; for another set of parents it might mean enrolling the child in a local treatment program. Still another parent might choose private counseling and a fourth set of parents might choose to involve the child in a rigorous program of activities including work, family counseling, individual counseling and close monitoring and supervision by the parents and other adults. Another parent might put the child out of the home.

As you read the list of options available to the parents in the example above, did you feel anything? If not, go back and read them again and watch for an emotional or physical reaction to the choices presented. One or more of those options felt good to you. That is the feeling you are looking for when you are at the second step in the process of practicing integrity. The choice made may be difficult and one may need help carrying it out. However, if it is the right action, it will relieve anxiety and bring peace. The wrong action will not relieve anxiety. Instead, it may result in years of guilt feelings and emotional pain.

INTEGRITY: HOW TO PRACTICE IT

Tools are available to help us find the course of integrity. When each of us uses the tools, we receive our own individual answer. The process introduced below takes you to your center. That essence within you which knows everything is waiting to tell you whatever you need to know. The process takes you to your Source, the Essence of your being, and gives you a stethoscope through which to hear It speak — loudly and clearly, like a heartbeat. After repeatedly using one or more of the tools suggested below, you will come to recognize the feeling in your body that goes along, or resonates, with the revelation of your individual course of integral action. At that point, you may not need to stop and use a tool; you may only have to listen to your body for the feeling that you know accompanies the right choice for your personal action.

THE TOOLS

Throughout this volume, four tools will be used to signal yes or no answers to questions raised in the 7-Step Process. These tools have been selected because of their familiarity and therefore your ease in visualizing them. For those who have trouble with visualization, the tools are reproduced on the following page. The tools are as follows:

1. **A traffic light**—Assign green to represent a "YES" response; red is a definite "NO!"

2. **A huge thermometer**—All of the bright red mercury is below the lines of gradation used for measurement. The highest point on the thermometer represents a "YES" response. If the mercury only rises a short distance, that is not a definitive "YES". You may modify the question to seek a stronger response. If the mercury in your thermometer does not rise, that represents a resounding "NO" response to your question.

3. **A big light bulb**—The bulb lights when your answer is "YES." It remains dark, or dead, when the answer to your question is "NO." Dimly lit bulbs suggest there is some merit to the question but not enough to warrant a resounding "Yes." Once again, you may try to modify the question to achieve a stronger response.

4. **A large clock**—The ticking of the clock becomes louder and louder as you move closer to a "YES" response. The ticking is loudest when you have reached the strongest integrity position for you.

The reader is reminded that the tools should always be used in concert with listening to the body to learn your body's response, that is, what you feel, that corresponds with the messages from the tools. In this way we can become attuned to our bodies' messages and eventually, will only use the tools when we want to weigh very carefully a more complex issue.

The 7-Step Process for Practicing Integrity

Part 1: Knowing what is right to do or not do

The first thing one has to do in the practice of integrity is know the right thing to do or not do. There are four steps in this part of the process:

Step 1:	**Sit quietly. Take a few deep abdominal breaths. Drop the shoulders; loosen the jaw; relax.**
Step 2:	**Form your question(s) about what is right.** For example: The accountant in my office is stealing funds. Should I do something? Should I "mind my own business" and do nothing?
Step 3:	**Visualize one of the following tools:** a. **A traffic light.** Assign green to represent the right course of action; red is a definite "NO!" b. **A huge thermometer.** All of the bright red mercury is below the lines of gradation. The highest point on the thermometer represents the right action for you. c. **A big light bulb.** The bulb lights when your answer is yes. d. **A large clock.** The ticking of the clock becomes louder and louder as you move closer to the right action for you. The ticking is loudest when you have reached the answer which represents your truth.
Step 4:	**While visualizing the tool you have selected, ask each of the questions you face, such as the questions in the example at Step 2, and wait for your tool to give you your answer. You will also *feel* that the answer is right.**

Part II. How to do the right thing

There are three steps in this *second* part of the process for practicing integrity. This is the action-taking Part. It is likely the scariest and hardest to complete. However, to know what is right to do and *not* find a way to do it means that integrity is not being practiced.

Step 5: **Think of all of your options for action to carry out the answer you received from Step 4 above.**
In our example of the cheating accountant, let's assume your answer was, "Yes, do something." Your options might be:

a. Place an anonymous phone call to a board member
b. Leave an anonymous note on the desk of the executive director/CEO
c. Confront the accountant; give him a chance to rectify his misdeeds
d. Cover for the accountant and make up the shortages because he's in a crisis and told you about it
e. Call the accountant's best friend and ask the friend to talk to him
f. Etc., etc.

Step 6: **Run each option through your mind as you visualize your tool. Observe the reaction of your tool. If you get a definitive, high quality answer, go on to Step 7. If you don't get a high quality, definitive "yes" answer, give yourself more time to come up with additional options (Step 5) and take them back through Step 6.**

Step 7: **Move on your right action.** Remember that it's *your* answer and may not be the answer your spouse, parent, or friend would have received. Don't let others' opinions keep you from acting on your right action.

You will also *feel* this answer is right for you if you listen to your body.

RELATED CONCEPTS

Sometimes other words and concepts are used interchangeably with "integrity." This can cause confusion when one is trying to practice integrity. The popular interpretation of some of these terms and the differences between them and integrity are discussed below.

HONESTY

"Honesty" is defined in the source[6] for this book as:

(1) probity; uprightness; integrity - each of these words is used as a synonym for the other. Honesty is further defined as

(2) truthfulness, sincerity, or frankness and

(3) freedom from deceit or fraud .

I think of "honesty" as telling the truth, and not stealing. To have integrity, we must do both of those things and more. Integrity requires adherence to a standard of moral conduct in other actions besides speaking the truth and taking what is not our own. Consequently, one is not considered to have integrity if one is *just* honest. But, one cannot have integrity if one is *not* honest.

ACCOUNTABILITY

From Webster's,[6] accountability is the noun for the adjective, "account + able" and therefore is the characteristic of being responsible, answerable. We cannot have integrity and not be responsible for ourselves and our actions. We have to hold ourselves, individually, answerable for the actions taken and claim them as our own. Accountability is not integrity, but we cannot practice integrity without taking responsibility for our actions. To take responsibility, we have to acknowledge the actions are our own and not the cause of or caused by any other person, circumstance or force. Taking full responsibility for our actions and inactions gives one power over one's life. It's a "take charge" attitude.

LOYALTY

"Loyalty" is defined[6] as "...faithfulness to commitments or obligations and synonyms are "fealty, devotion, constancy." Unlike other terms we consider here, loyalty comes with emotionalism attached. The term loyalty implies a sense of duty or devoted attachment. Therein lies the danger to the practice of integrity in situations involving loyalty. The loyalty versus integrity dilemma pops up most notably in employee-employer situations but can occur in all human relationships. Certainly, exposing the company's wrong-doing, or that of a colleague or our own (albeit on behalf of the company), is not going to be appreciated by the company and may create hardship for the employee.

The dilemma could present itself as the choice between engaging in amoral conduct on behalf of the company or taking the high ground. Before making the choice, the individual often agonizes and vacillates between the two. The reason for the agony is the knowing — we know the right thing to do, but don't know how to do the right thing in a way that is easy and least hurtful to ourselves or the entity to which we are loyal.

ETHICAL BEHAVIOR

"Ethics" (singular or plural) is defined[6] as 1) a system of moral principles; 2) the rules of conduct recognized in respect to a particular class of human actions or a particular group, culture, etc.; 3) moral principles, as of an individual; and 4) that branch of philosophy dealing with values relating to human conduct with respect to the rightness and wrongness of certain actions and to the goodness and badness of the motives and ends of such actions. By extension, then, "ethical behavior" would be that behavior which is in concert with the 'system of moral principles,' the recognized 'rules of conduct' or one's 'moral principles.' These definitions, especially the third one relating to the individual, surprised me and caused me to look up morals.

"Morals" is defined[6] as "principles or habits with respect to right or wrong conduct." My surprise stems from my impression, based on my observation of the usage of the term "ethics" in popular discourse, that the term referred to standards of conduct based on an interpretation of laws written by humans. These stan-

dards might apply to the laws and regulations in a particular profession or to a sector. However, in most cases the focus appeared
to me to be upon how to interpret the law to avoid lawsuits and
challenges to a person's license or professional skill.

I took a mini straw poll, asking others about the meaning of
ethics and the teaching of ethics. Each thought as I did. One suggested that it used to be that ethics meant personal honesty as sig-
nified by a handshake representing an agreement. Now, however, that person said, the teaching of ethics focuses on how to
manipulate the law to one's advantage without being sued.
Perhaps, at one time, integrity and ethicalness could have been
used as synonyms. Now, however, I argue that their meanings
diverge in significant ways as shown in the following diagram.

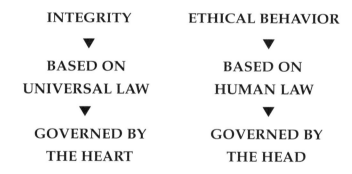

INTEGRITY	ETHICAL BEHAVIOR
▼	▼
BASED ON	BASED ON
UNIVERSAL LAW	HUMAN LAW
▼	▼
GOVERNED BY	GOVERNED BY
THE HEART	THE HEAD

Integrity—Our Definition

So, just what is integrity? What exactly do we mean when we
say "integrity?" We opened this chapter with that question. I
believe it can be quite simply put in these words we have all
likely heard before.

**Integrity is doing the right thing – in thought, word (writ-
ten and spoken) and action.**

To practice integrity successfully, you have to first know what
is right and second, know how to do the right thing in the easiest
way for you.

CHAPTER 2:
Personal Integrity

The previous chapter explains what integrity is, how to know it and how to use tools to assist the practice of personal integrity. That information is basic to everything to be discussed from here forward. If you skipped Chapter 1, go back. Nothing else I say will make sense to you if you don't.

PERSONAL INTEGRITY

KEY TO ACHIEVING INTEGRITY IN ALL OF LIFE

Acting with integrity in any other role (parent, spouse, business person, client, staff person, chief executive officer, governor) requires one to return to personal (individual) integrity. That is the foundation for all other relationships: a board of directors is made up of individuals; employees are individuals, corporate partners are, first of all, individuals. England's House of Commons is made up of individuals; the Native American Tribal Council members are individuals first. If we learn personal integrity and can respond to personal issues from a place of integrity, we can take that practice into a performance appraisal meeting, the Board Room, a child's bedroom, the marital bed, the

Congress of the United States. When we are practicing integrity, we can and will require it of others. We, the world public, can change the direction of world spin.

Personal integrity is the key to the practice of integrity at all levels in every situation. It all starts and ends with the individual. Practicing personal integrity is not predicated on whether or not someone is looking. It is taking the high road even if nobody is looking, nobody could possibly discover the indiscretion and everybody you know would take the low road. Practicing integrity is not a Sunday behavior, reserved for the day you visit your mom or for the first week you are on your new job. Personal integrity is an every day, all day, anywhere behavior. As the popular saying goes, it is a 24-7/365 thing.

Wayne Dyer tells the story of his practice of gratefulness.[7] He offers a few words of thanksgiving for small things like courtesies extended in traffic or in parking lots, for beautiful days, for rainy days. Basically, he expresses gratitude for little things all day, every day. Practicing integrity is the same way: run your decisions and options by your visual tool all day, every day, for little things and big.

In marriage, each spouse brings baggage. You don't get to be an adult and not have accumulated some baggage. Even if you have not done formal psychological work, learning to operate your life from a position of integrity can stop you from foisting some of that baggage onto your partner. It's easier if you have the habit of relating to the world with integrity. When we enter a new relationship (with in-laws, new friends, step-children) we more easily apply our tools to the new situation. People dealt with honestly and openly, with integrity, feel valued and more empowered. Building good relationships is easier.

INTEGRITY WITH THE SELF *

People who sacrifice themselves will always be called upon to be sacrificial. If we have "outgrown" that role, we feel put upon, angry and persecuted if we continue to play that role. Those feelings are the first clues that it's time to drop the lamb's coat because we are out of integrity with the Self. Our Inner Voice is not being heard and we will not be happy if we continue in this role. People will expect us to be the sacrificial lamb as long as we allow ourselves to be in that role. Only the individual can call a halt to it.

When I was 43, I moved 3000 miles away from all 10 members of my family of origin and hundreds of aunts, uncles, cousins, nieces and nephews. I said my "good government job" held little interest, and the low-cost, excellent quality educational system where I was going would make college for my daughter financially easier for me, now a single mother. In addition, I cited a growing difficulty with cold, East Coast winters due to a circulatory condition. About 10 years later, I realized that what I'd really moved away from was my role in my family of origin. As the eldest daughter, second child of nine, I had been the caretaker and mother's helper from an early age since I showed capacity to accept and discharge responsibility well. As an adult, I was the organizer of events and activities and the ear of choice and architect of options and solutions when there was a problem. In return, I hardly ever had to pay for handyman services. One or more of my seven brothers was always there. If one of them could not do it — whatever it was — they knew someone who could.

When I left all of this support system, I suddenly realized I was really on my own. Over the years I was away from home, I became my own person — the real person I am to express in the world. I'm not very different from the person I expressed at the

---

* Self (capitalized) refers to the essence of who one is. It is that part of a person that is connected to every other part of creation and the Creator. It is the place in each of us that is all knowing; the part of each of us that is Infinite. In this book, I interchangeably use the terms "Self," "the heart" and "one's Center." The terms "oneself," ourselves," "yourself," (all lower case) refer to the ego-self. That is, the way we think we are; the person we see; the limited, physical, mental being. (Adapted from definitions provided in The Wholeness Handbook, by Emuth & Greenhut, MD. New York: The Continuum Publishing Co., 1991)

age of 16 to 21; yet I'm very different. I am a lot like the 43-year old I was when I left; but I'm nothing like the person I was then. During high school and college, I was a much sought after leader and a skilled public speaker. Today, I easily say no to leadership positions; but I still love public speaking. When I left home, I was an Episcopalian who believed in the sanctity of all religions because God by any name is still omnipotent and everywhere present. Today, I am a metaphysician who believes that Spirit by any name is still the only Power and that all matter is an expression of that Power which connects us, inextricably, to our environment and each other. As a unique expression of that Power, each of us has a unique purpose and work to do on this planet.

I used to believe in the old saw, "You can't go home again." I found that I can go home, and I did — nearly 13 years after leaving — because I had changed. I know who I am and work at keeping my integrity with my Self. I try to relate to family members with total integrity. I speak my mind with humor and warmth, but firmly. I express my expectations, goals and priorities and I work on **my** priorities. In fairness to my family members, while I've been gone, they have changed — grown and developed — and they follow their own life courses. We're much more a collection of leaders of our own Selves.

I don't know if everyone has to literally go away to do what I did, but I know if I hadn't made that change in my life, I would be one of those angry, self-sacrificing persons who was made ill by my inner rage. Developing integrity with my Self and practicing it daily has made me happier and healthier.

Personal integrity is the claiming of individual authority. Every individual has authority over his or her thoughts, actions and feelings. No one can think, act or feel for another. Acting with personal integrity shows the exercise of that God-given right to reason and express in words, actions and thoughts as only that one individual can. By claiming individual authority, one leads his/her own life, in spite of the opinions of others, separate and apart from what others do, feel or think. By claiming individual authority we acknowledge the essence of who we are. It is, at once, the greatest gift and the greatest responsibility we have to exercise in our lifetimes.

Not long ago, I was accosted by a man who lived next door to me. My first reaction to the attack was extreme anger, followed by frustration at having re-injured my knee in the struggle (I was on crutches at the time). After calling friends for support, I slid into a tub of warm, bubbly water where I asked the question: "What is the lesson here? What is the Universe trying to tell me?" I got my answers and knew they were right because of a feeling I get when I get answers. A week later, my strongest emotion was still anger, even after seeing a psychologist to talk about it and seeing an orthopedic surgeon to have the new pain in my knee assessed. Soon after, I realized anger had been the prevailing emotion for too long. I had gotten the information from the incident, so I needed to thank "the messenger" and give him what he was asking for from me. His karma led him to this experience because he need-ed to have the repercussions to learn his lessons. I had already filed the police report and I now knew I needed to press charges to the full extent of the law. The outcome of that action, one year pro-bation and some financial impact, is what that individual needed.

In this way I exercised my individual authority. I considered my options. I **chose** to give up the negative emotions around the experience. I **chose** to reject putting up barriers and closing down my heart. I **chose** not to have friends retaliate against the man as many of them wanted to do. I **chose** to get on with my life. That was practicing personal integrity for me. Those decisions and actions gave me peace and a good feeling about myself, as well.

Some of you, especially women who have had similar ordeals, may think that I simply shrugged off what was a terrifying and hurtful experience. It may sound that way. But I went through a process to get to this place. The message I received from the inci-dent was life changing. I could not move on to the joy which awaited me in my new life if I stayed stuck in the emotions from that negative experience. I had a cross-country move to arrange and I gave myself the healing journey of driving myself leisurely across the country. In the meantime, I held to my resolve to see the legal process through even though I was now thousands of miles way. And the legal process took months – which gave me even more time and additional opportunities to revisit the emotions and vent.

Each individual is different from every other individual— even one's identical twin. Each born in a different space and time, is the expression of his/her own Potential. Each is endowed with a complex of skills, insights, talents, creativity, intelligence, likes and dislikes. To truly be oneself, each individual must be an expression of that complexity — honestly and lovingly. To be in integrity with the Self, the individual has to listen to the heart within. Sometimes called intuition, this force is the voice of the soul... the voice of integrity. It is easy to hear; we only have to listen. **Part 1** in the process of practicing integrity causes us to listen. When we follow the messages we get from that Source, we are in integrity with the Self.

Our role on the planet is to discover the universe of what we are, discover how to love who we are and give that special something expression in the world. In the process, each of us must recognize that every other individual has a similar complex of attributes and is expressing that specialness in the world. Therefore, to practice integrity in one's personal life, the individual has to honor (give voice to) one's own uniqueness while at the same time respecting the voice/expression/being of every other individual. Such a requirement creates challenge in the individual's relationship with the Self, one's life partner, children, co-workers and friends, indeed with the entire universe. This is not easy to do. However, the results are worth the effort.

OWNING YOUR OWN POWER

The opening line in M. Scott Peck's *The Road Less Traveled*[8] is "Life is difficult." If you accept that as a premise, your life work becomes figuring out how to make life easier. Or, in other words, you become focused on learning each lesson as it presents itself so you don't have to keep repeating the same "class" which the Universe makes more difficult and with heavier consequences until we finally "get it." Once you accept your power to make your life easier, you begin to look for the lessons in every situation, especially the difficult situations, because you know you must have missed this lesson when it came around before.

In the Fall of 1998, I attended a mass and healing service at the Roman Catholic Church in which I grew up. The Peruvian priest who was officiating, announced that it was the Feast of the Exalted Cross (Spanish) or Feast of the Holy Crucifix (English). He discussed the role of pain in our lives. "Pain is to draw us closer to Christ," he said. "When we surrender our will, only then do we come closer to God. The pain enables us to wake up to God; He gets our attention. God can lift the pain, but he wants us in return."[9]

That's the power I'm talking about. We have the power to choose to give up our conviction that we know it all (mentally and intellectually) and surrender to our hearts, which truly do know it all. The Inner Voice of the soul will tell us what's right, how to do what's right and how to get the peace and ease we are looking for. The 7-Step Process introduced in Chapter 1 is simply an aid to hearing the Inner Voice.

LIVING YOUR LIFE PURPOSE

Each individual is a unique expression of a divine energy source. Each individual is on this journey called "life" with a destination. While on this journey, one's unique purpose will also be completed. That purpose could be giving birth to and raising a world leader, saving a small child from a rushing current, being a caring adult for a neighborhood child who needs some extra love or adding beauty through a poem or a piece of art. Whatever it is, no one else can write that specific poem or help that specific child just that special way except the one whose purpose it is. Many individuals struggle to figure out what their work is; many times we are looking for lofty, highly visible, earth-shaking roles and overlook the important work we do every day.

At 80, my mother spent many hours in prayer and contemplation. She was a devout Catholic and attended Mass daily. She has lit enough candles and prayed enough novenas to save the world. Every time there was some ripple in the family, our Mom was holding the situation in prayer. Sometimes she prayed for a specific outcome and she got frustrated when she didn't get that outcome. Then she backed off and asked for *the* perfect outcome. And while the perfect outcome was never what she expected or wanted, it was usually better than the outcome for which she originally prayed. She would tell us how hard she was praying for some particular outcome for one of us in a way that it sounded like an onerous thing. It made my siblings and me feel guilty about causing her to be "on her knees, again!" as we jokingly complained to one another. Then a funny thing happened. We noticed that her prayers were being answered... with a "Yes!" We started calling her to tell her what to pray for. Most of the time she had beat us to it, having already discerned that the situation needed prayer. My Mom's life purpose, at 80, could have been her prayer work.

One is practicing integrity when one stands firm in the conviction to pursue what is felt at a deep level to be one's life purpose. The Universe will respond with support. Standing firm requires the patient suffering of others' doubts and attacks on our mental competence. Standing firm requires moving forward on faith knowing the Universe is a co-conspirator for good. Sometimes, it is frightening to learn what our work is. We always have choices; we can choose not to do our work. But walking away from one's purpose diminishes the expression of the Divine in the world. When we overcome our fear and step into our work, the Universe conspires to support us. That support may appear in the form of the alleviation of the fear, presentation of the resources needed to do the work or the appearance of a helper.

When our life purpose is not known, it is even more important to keep doing all we can do to live life fully, learning all the lessons from life's curves and fouls and winning moments. Each of us must know that the "what" will be revealed when we are ready. Until that revelation occurs, we are "in training."

INTEGRITY WITH ONESELF

SPEAKING ONE'S MIND

Speaking up is a way of showing up. We are often called upon to speak out against actions which lack integrity. We can speak out with words or through actions planned, contemplated and carried out. These occasions occur in one-on-one situations, among small groups of friends or family members, in the Board room, at power breakfasts and in places of worship. They occur within our homes, our legislatures and on the Little League ball field. They occur among our most intimate associates and in the company of strangers. The action we take determines whether we actually *practice integrity*.

RACISM, SEXISM and OTHER PREJUDICE

"Your freedom ends where the tip of my nose begins" is not really about physical location and protrusion of body parts. It is about the person-hood of another. Our individual freedom ends where another's humanity begins. The race, religion, sex, economic strata, or state of another's mental or physical soundness is coincidental to his/her humanhood — just like height and eye color. It is not our responsibility to approve or to not approve of those characteristics. None of them has anything to do with us.

None of us has totally escaped the sting of prejudice. At the same time, all of us express prejudice in one way or another. People who are *consistently* subjected to prejudice feel it rather quickly when in the presence of another or in an environment where it exists. While we are often accused of paranoia, in truth we are usually picking up on an energy present in our surroundings. Many of us who have experienced pervasive prejudice simply keep on walking, doing what is ours to do in the world without regard to the opinions of others. Our prejudices are just that — our opinions! Our stuff! This does not make it okay for others to have to struggle through our "stuff." Our stuff is ours. It is our struggle to overcome since it comes from our irrational fears of lack and limitation: "They'll take all the jobs." "They aren't smart enough to do this work as well as men." "They belong at home." "They are too old; their skills are rusty." "They might have AIDS and cause my health insurance to go up." Your stuff causes you to put up physical and material blocks. Your stuff gets in their way... and *yours*...because prejudice may slow down the persecuted, but it will stall the prejudiced one permanently. Two sayings I've heard since I was a child make the point well:

> "You can't keep one foot on my throat and move ahead yourself."

> "To hold me down in the gutter you have to stay there with me."

This is not an "American problem." I have not heard of a society where there is no ethnic or sexual prejudice. If each individual, one person at a time, stopped supporting the particular prejudice in his society and her own personal circle, it would crumble. We have only to look at the fall of the Berlin Wall in Germany and the fall of communism as the official government in the Union of Soviet Socialist Republics to realize how fast the individuals of a given social structure can bring down mighty structures which lack integrity. We almost saw it again at Tiananmen Square when students challenged the Chinese government.

CHAPTER 3:
Integrity In Leadership—Civil Servants

SEXUAL HARASSMENT

Defining and dealing with sexual harassment is one of the greatest dilemmas of our times. Many men believe the growing movement of women toward equality has made them less feminine. Yet, men continue to regard women as sex objects. Some men think their attentions should be seen as flattery and that women really do want the attention even if they say they don't. Women are just as guilty of harassing men by constantly flirting, indicating they are always available, or persistently calling and requesting a man's company. Many men give in to this unsolicited attention. Few men complain. Sexual harassment, however, is *any* unwanted sexual attention – whether it be from males or females.

What makes this issue so volatile is that you cannot tell what any one person will consider harassment at any given time. As the laws have been strengthened to protect people, many individuals are being charged and punished for doing what was "okay" before. "Okay" simply means the victims never had recourse before. Now they do. And less often are they seen as being responsible for or as inviting the problem. In fact, the treatment of victims in this arena has changed so much that now the victim is assumed right and the accused has to prove innocence.

The key phrase for all of us to remember is *unwanted* sexual attention, whether it is a look, advance, touch, word, picture, joke— anything. If unwanted, it is harassment. So if the other person lets you know by body language, verbally or by any other means that your words or actions are not welcome, you are required to honor that person's wishes to be in integrity... and to avoid a lawsuit.

TAKING ADVANTAGE OF THE EMPLOYER (THE PUBLIC)

An integrity issue faces those who work for government agencies. These agencies' funds belong to and come from members of the public. We, the public, expect these funds to be spent well. Just as we have to manage our own homes and financial affairs with due diligence, we expect the same from you who work to provide services to us.   There are many instances, day-to-day, where employees misuse public funds through:

- Excessive use of agency phone lines to make personal calls
- Taking agency supplies home for personal use
- Long, personal conversations with co-workers on agency time
- Overly long lunch hours
- Fabricating or overstating costs on expense reports
- Inaccurately reporting time on time sheets
- Working overtime when tasks could have been completed during the normal workday
- Giving less than an honest day's work for a day's wage on a consistent basis

I am not advocating isolationism. Building relationships in the workplace helps to get the work done.   Everyone has a day here and there when interruptions, the news story of the day, or something internal to the office destroys concentration.   I am not encouraging guilt or tension. I am encouraging moderation and sensitivity to our responsibility to the members of the public who pay our salaries.

PLAYING FAVORITES IN FUNDING

In conferring grant and contract awards, deciding officials have great power. We can exercise integrity in those decisions or we can use the perceived power of those money awards for other purposes than intended by the authority providing the funds. Staff members spend months to prepare the grant or contract application guidelines, making clear the needs of the funding agency and the purposes for which grants or contracts will be awarded. Significant resources are expended in recruiting a group of experts in the fields in which grant awards will be made, assuring a lack of conflict of interest for these readers and raters of written applications. The peer review findings are obtained, and together with staff comments, the applications are forwarded in rank order to the deciding official. A decision by the official to award grants outside of the rank order should be defensible. That is, it should be easy for staff to explain to applicants, who have competed at great cost to themselves, that the program's goals could not have been met if proposals had been funded in rank order. Furthermore, an explanation of how the program goals are compromised is appropriate and staff should be empowered to provide the explanation. Such honesty and directness promote confidence in the process, the specific agency and its leadership.

DE-EMPHASIZING THE TRUTH

"We are not lying. We are just de-emphasizing the truth." This is the explanation given by some corporate entities and government agencies for what is done when there is information that is too bad to make public. When they know the information would cause panic, or worse, lawsuits, agency representatives often de-emphasize the truth.

There are several ways to de-emphasize the truth. For example, a study of conditions might be done and when the report comes back with its very dangerous findings, the client agency orders the study report redone or suppresses the report altogether. When the agency requires reports to be altered, the contractor is provided an opportunity to practice integrity. If the report is not altered, the contractor may not get paid for the job. If contractor staff refuse to alter the report, in spite of the contractor's usual compliance with such requests, that individual might certainly lose his or her job.

If the alteration of the report is done, it might take one of the following forms:

- Raising the minimum level for safety and/or extending the maximum level for safety so that the findings fit within the "safe" zone.

- Using colors in the report that are not associated with danger. For example, graphs or charts done in gradients of brown are less alarming than graphs or charts done in red.

This integrity issue involves both government and businesses. Suggestions in Section II are meant to help civil servants identify options which have greater integrity with the public they serve.

WHISTLE BLOWING

Two hundred years ago, the workers' task was simply to provide the best possible service to the customers — all valued sources of revenue — or incur the wrath of the owner. The business owner was the conscience of the worker. With the change in the goal and character of today's business from benevolent neighbor to often impersonal, multi-national, investor-focused entity, the role of the worker has also changed. Now the worker is often called upon to be the conscience of the corporation. The whistle blower is the one who is experiencing a call to practice integrity. Regardless of the laws protecting whistle blowers, these individuals seldom recover from the events surrounding their heroic practice of integrity. As whistle blowers, we may not lose our jobs, but we often exist in a hell of hostility. Our futures are ruined. We must find the courage to make a new life. We all benefit from the personal pain and punishment of whistle blowers. We owe each of them a huge "Thank You!" Few examples of practicing integrity exact such a great cost. This example, however, serves to point up the fact that the practice of integrity is neither always easy nor always appreciated. But, it does always make society more whole.

PROMOTIONS AND AWARDS

Governments generally have a system of rewards and recognition for employees who distinguish themselves. The size of the award depends upon the impact of the achievement. Promotions are used in the same way. Here's the rub. Often favoritism, racism, sexism and other "isms" are practiced in the award/promotion system. One employee may receive a cash award while another receives a promotion for similar accomplishments or for *no* special accomplishments. The employee who receives the promotion is being favored since the promotion pays that employee every year from that time forward at a higher rate — quickly outpacing the amount of the one-time cash award given the other employee.

Since the employee receiving the award does not like to appear ungrateful, he or she often sits and grows more and more resentful watching co-workers climb the promotional ladder. Supervisors practicing integrity will not allow such a situation to occur in their areas of responsibility.

CHAPTER 4:
Integrity In Leadership—
Elected and Appointed Officials

There is probably no area of life where we want integrity more but expect it less than among elected officials. There is probably no area of life where integrity is *needed* more but *evidenced* less than among elected officials. Many politicians are lawyers and that compounds the problem. We, in the United States of America, have a love-hate relationship with the legal profession. Everybody wants to find good lawyers when they need them. But nobody can stand them *until* they need one.

Everybody wants to trust what politicians say; but experience has taught us they will say anything to get our vote. Everybody wants to vote for someone who values what they value, but when it comes right down to it, we know that when the deals are being made in the backrooms or on the golf courses, and when the mutual back scratching starts, what we value may be sold away for something else. All of this puts us through manic-depressive-type mood swings toward our elected governmental officials.

Appointed officials, on the other hand, don't feel the same burden of responsibility to us as do elected officials. Appointed officials, rather, feel some responsibility to act in line with the values of the person who appointed them. There is no problem with that. We would expect that. That's why most of us recognize the importance of electing someone to public office who will appoint judges, commissioners, regents of educational institutions and special assistants who reflect our values. The question of integrity I raise for appointed officials has to do with the responsibility they *do have* to the public as well as to the person who appointed them.

The specific integrity issues discussed in this chapter are as follows:

1. Animosity between branches of government
2. Unbridled partisanship and use of smoke screens
3. Selling the vote
4. Wasting money/Pork barrels
5. Lopsided treaties and trade agreements
6. Misuse of and disrespect for international organizations
7. Responsibility to the people

ANIMOSITY BETWEEN BRANCHES OF GOVERNMENT

I have watched the animosity between the legislative (Congress) and executive (President and Cabinet Departments) branches of government in the United States of America grow over the last two decades to a point where I believe the attack/counter-attack strategies are destroying these two institutions of government. The charge to protect the Constitution of the United States is a very important one. Our elected officials know that goal will get our support. Right now, however, that charge is being used to justify actions which are derogatory and demeaning toward the institutions of the presidency and the Congress. It will take a long time for our institutions to rise again to their pre-1992 level of respect in our own and in world opinion.

The following example makes the point.

It is one thing to collect information on a sitting president, weigh the culpability, and bring that president up for impeachment if there is cause. I would never argue with that role of Congress. It is a part of the system of checks and balances that ensures no branch of government oversteps its boundaries. It is one example of the brilliance of the architects of the current national structure. It assures no one person or branch of government becomes too powerful. But what the 106th Congress did was abdicate its responsibility in the presidential impeachment process in late 1998. We, the public, paid for a multi-million dollar investigation that extended over four years. (On February 3, 1999, *The Washington Post* reported costs to date for the Starr investigations of $40 million.) The investigation found that President Bill Clinton had engaged in adultery and may or may not have lied about it. He may or may not have asked others to lie about it. So, at best, the investigation was inconclusive about the obstruction of justice charges that were the basis for impeachment. So what did the Congress do next? It put all of its raw data on the Internet and into the hands of the people of the world and said, "You decide."

While Mr. Clinton's behavior was reprehensible and an embarrassment to all of us, the Congress might have sought other options for carrying out their responsibility rather than relying on public opinion to determine their next actions. The Congress allowed its hostility for the man in the White House to blind it to appropriate execution of its duty. Both institutions – the presidency and the Congress – have been diminished by this episode. On September 22, 1998, the delegates of the United Nations gave Bill Clinton, the President of the United States of America, a standing ovation.[10] They gave him that ovation because they recognized the depth to which the legislative branch of government had sunk toward destroying the presidency; i.e., reducing the status of the office in the world community and possibly negatively affecting the incumbent's ability to execute the functions of that office.[11] There is no real defense for such actions. That's why Clinton received that ovation. That's why the revered and internationally respected Nelson Mandela, then President of South Africa, stood by his side. World leaders understood this. Our "leaders" did not.

Several other examples of institution destroying behavior deserve mention:

- Stalling legislative action on provisions important to the well-being of citizens in an effort to avoid credit going to the White House instead of the Congress;

- Vetoing legislation when done solely to avoid credit going to the Congress instead of the White House;

- Failing to reach agreement on an annual budget and;

- Failing to allow legislation favored by a majority of the elected officials in the Congress to leave committee for a vote.

These are all examples of the use of power by elected officials to diminish the effectiveness of branches of government.

UNBRIDLED PARTISANSHIP and USE OF SMOKE SCREENS

When we go to the polls and vote for individuals to represent us in the executive and legislative branches, we sometimes feel we are choosing between the lesser of two evils. I have heard it said many times by good citizens that while they feel it is their responsibility to vote, they also feel there is little difference between the candidates. But to hear the candidates talk, you would think they are saints and their opponents villains. In the Fall 1998 elections, for example, the mud slinging, name calling, accusations and counter accusations, lying about achievements and voting records, and violence reached an all time high.[12]

Thirty-six percent (36%) of eligible voters actually cast ballots. Since 1960 the percent of voting age population that participates in this part of the democratic process has been dropping. In the years in which we elect a president, we are down to less that 50% of those old enough to vote. In off year elections (when the presidency is not at stake) the numbers dropped to 38% in 1974 and have remained in the 36-38% range since then.[13] This backlash is likely to continue and to worsen if negative behavior on the part of candidates does not stop. It is too much work to figure out who's lying on whom and who's lying about what they did and didn't do. Citizens should not have to wade through this kind of muck and mire to exercise their voting rights.

Another example of unbridled partisanship occurs when commissions and departments of the executive branch are forced to operate for long periods of time without a leader that can design policy and guide its implementation. Approval actions on proposed candidates for those leadership positions languish on Capital Hill waiting for hearings to be scheduled. Some candidates actually have hearings but the atmosphere is hostile, the questioning focuses on narrow areas of past behavior and the hearings end in disapproval. These strategies seek to force the White House to withdraw the nomination, which prevents formation of a viable team and stalls the possible achievements of a given administration. It does not matter which major party controls Congress, this wasteful, partisan behavior is a way of life on Capital Hill. We are certainly not role models for the two-party system and the separation of powers. We are making a mockery of democracy *at the same time we try to convince other societies they should trade in their systems for ours.*

The *real* business of the Congress is often derailed by the obsession with party interests. The 1999 fiscal year budget became so larded with pet projects and fat, and so huge — nearly 4,000 pages thick — that even the members of Congress admitted freely that they didn't know what was in it and for what they were voting.[14] To their credit, some conservative members screamed and howled at the abuses. But in the end, the budget bill passed overwhelmingly in both houses of Congress and was signed without protest by the White House.

Both Congress and the White House loaded up the 1999 budget with everything under the sun to assure favorable 1998 election results. Would we, as a nation, have been better served if the commitment to the deficit-protection budget cap agreed to in 1997 had been honored? Would we have felt better knowing that we were voting for *real* leadership in the Fall 1998 election? Is that important to the people of this country? Yes. I dare say it is quite important. Once again, we deride corruption and mis-management in other governments at the same time we fail to model fiscal responsibility... and everyone is watching us.

SELLING THE VOTE

They tell me it's necessary to sell the vote so they can afford to run in the next election. Campaign costs have gotten so out of hand that candidates for elected office can only afford to enter the competition if they are wealthy or are very well known in their electoral districts. Current elected representatives can only afford to run again if they have been good enough to listen to political action committees (PACs), lobbyists for big business, and special interest groups (SIGs). So how good are these representatives for *us*? They say their vote is not affected by the gifts of money. I only want to ask our elected officials if *they* think *we* think those causes will continue to finance a "representative's" campaigns if the "representative" does not vote for their positions?

WASTING MONEY/PORK BARRELS

The ways in which our elected officials waste money are too numerous to mention. However, several areas have always seemed especially devoid of integrity and I will discuss them, briefly.

In our foreign policy, we provide aid where we have a political interest we want another country to serve. We have made multi-million dollar aid grants for transportation projects, aqueducts, energy plants, and similar infrastructure development programs. We will make those payments until the country is no longer of strategic importance to us. Then the money stops and millions of dollars worth of equipment and partially completed plants, roads, and railways stand rusting in the sun.

Similarly, we fund major projects in a hurry to beat other powers to claiming a particular ally. The funding flows even though it is obvious that the new ally does not have the skills and resources to maintain and manage the project once built. Five years later, we have done nothing to assure skills development or the development of a maintenance program and the project sits there falling apart year by year. In sharp contrast to this United States of America foreign aid practice, the Chinese and Cubans have worked shoulder to shoulder with other nationals to help them develop the skills to build and maintain the funded projects.

Another scenario is played out far too often. We have provided large sums of money to despots and tyrants for development of their countries. We know these funds only go into the personal coffers of these individuals. The "projects" we fund never come on line, but we keep providing money. In the process we create bigger, stronger monsters and more deprived citizens in these lands. In some landmark cases, these individuals have turned on us when it became in their best interest to do so — when it was no longer acceptable to have us call the marching orders.

Much closer to home, we waste far too much money. To reduce the size of government – a constant cry among Americans – government now contracts out for almost everything. We buy hundred dollar screwdrivers and pay far more per hour for a consultant than would be paid for an employee to do the same job. That should be insult enough to integrity. Add to that the fact that the government employee overseeing or monitoring a contract far too often does nothing to see that the project is being completed according to plan **and** budget. The size of cost overruns is legendary. Only when there are investigations into the high cost of contract work or fraud followed by jail sentences and fines do we get more appropriate costs **and** expenditures.[15] Essentially, what I am suggesting in this instance is that we are not good custodians of the resources provided by the citizens of this country. Government is out of integrity with those it purports to serve and for whom it is empowered to act.

As a nation, our financial house is certainly not in order. After decades of irresponsible spending, we have balanced the budget... for one year anyway. We owe our Social Security investment fund millions of dollars after having used those funds to bail us out in other areas over the years. The baby-boomers are about to go into retirement pushing onto Social Security rolls millions of individuals who will live longer than any generation before them. Our elected officials spent months, during the Year 2000 budget process, trying to decide how to spend the "surplus" which doesn't even exist yet. And, if that weren't bad enough, they want to cut taxes rather than using tax revenue to pay off some of our debt.

In the long run, paying down the debt would make us a stronger nation. In the short run, the tax cut may get some representatives more votes. The question should be, "What would be in the better interest of the country?" But that question gets pushed aside.

Our national budget every year is rife with barrels of "pork." We citizens should be outraged because *Webster's Encyclopedic Unabridged Dictionary of the English Language*[6] defines "pork barrel" as a government appropriation, bill or policy which supplies funds for local improvements designed to ingratiate legislators with their constituents. "Pork" is defined as appropriations, appointments, etc., made by the government for political reasons rather than for public benefit. In other words, *we* are being bought! These expenditures mean waste since the expenditure is for political reasons rather than the public good.

An excellent example showed up in the Washington newspapers and on the 60 Minutes TV program in late 1998. During preparation in Congress of the 1999 budget, Newt Gingrich, then Speaker of the House of Representatives, represented the area of Georgia where Lockheed Martin makes the C-130J cargo aircraft. Gingrich put a number of these planes into the budget after calling the Pentagon and asking why there was none in the Pentagon's budget. After hearing the reason, he proceeded to suggest they put these multi-million dollar planes in the budget because the funding would help Lockheed Martin's research and development on the next generation of these planes and keep the assembly lines rolling. Translation: keep his constituents employed. When the revised Pentagon budget showed up with only one (1) C-130, the Speaker increased the number to four (4); others were added by other players in the budget development process and on June 24, 1998 the House approved $431,000,000 worth of airplanes never requested by the Pentagon and at the expense of replacing aging craft as the Pentagon *had* requested.[16] To their credit, some outraged members of the House of Representatives called for a halt to such "pork."

A subsequent *Washington Post* article,[16] noted that this was the twenty-second year that the Congress has forced the Air Force to buy more new C-130 military transport aircraft than it wanted, changing Pentagon spending priorities and retiring previously purchased C-130s prematurely. Over this period, the Pentagon had only requested five (5) of the 256 that have been purchased for it. Georgia Congressional representatives and Congressional appropriations committees have forced the expenditures for more than two decades! This is just one example of many. All represent waste.

Wastes occur in every department of the Executive Branch as well as on Capitol Hill. If we summoned our will to practice integrity, we could begin to exercise fiscal responsibility and relinquish the title as the largest debtor nation in the community of nations.

LOPSIDED TREATIES AND TRADE AGREEMENTS

I used to wonder why it took years to get a trade agreement accepted and signed by the intended signatories. The presidents of the participating countries visit and meet and discuss. More years go by and finally, there is a signature amid much celebration here in the United States of America. Back in the early 1980's I was excited about the Caribbean Basin Initiative (CBI). I was recruited by associates in Miami to assist with clients in the region covered by the Initiative. Together, my colleagues and I went to hearings and briefings on Capitol Hill designed to assist those of us wanting to do business under the provisions of the Initiative. To my great surprise, with all the posturing in the American press about the advantages to the Caribbean, many of the provisions of that Initiative worked against the Caribbean states and favored us. They were not given *easy* access to our markets at all; tariffs and other fees were levied on their exports to us. But, our goods were not taxed going into their markets. We had spent years wearing them down, one country at a time. We try to sell these agreements as first steps with changes to come in future agreements.

Now, 15 years later, Caribbean nations operating under the CBI are being negatively affected by the North American Fair Trade Agreement (NAFTA). The lower duty required on goods from Mexico is attracting manufacturers in the Caribbean and causing them to relocate in Mexico. Caribbean nations are asking for parity with Mexico but cannot get their concerns addressed because of political enmity between the White House and the Congress. If those nations have been able to make this Initiative work for them, in spite of the Initiative's structural problems, then we should not want to see their gains eroded.

Now, an African nations trade agreement is being discussed by heads of state. Well-known analyst and researcher, Ron Walters (University of Maryland, Political Science Department), says this treaty is the same old thing. The financial gains are one-sided in favor of Americans. Duty is charged on African goods. Also African countries with relationships with certain other African countries would not be eligible to participate; participating African countries' economies would be subject to International Monetary Fund (IMF) restructuring requirements. Such requirements have been devastating to developing countries and have not had the "intended" result. This has been shown repeatedly.[17] We have to achieve integrity in our dealings with other countries.

MISUSE OF and DISRESPECT FOR INTERNATIONAL ORGANIZATIONS

Misuse of and/or disrespect for international peace-keeping and financial assistance organizations occurs when some countries (1) use their veto power inappropriately; (2) use the World Bank and International Monetary Fund to control the economies of smaller states; (3) maneuver issues outside of the appropriate international body; and (4) violate the spirit and intent of diplomatic agreements, thus under-cutting and destroying diplomatic solutions. A few examples of these issues follow:

Veto Power: United Nations - Only five nations, in the community of 185 members have the power to stop the body from discussing an issue, from voting on an issue, or from seeking diplomatic resolutions to an issue. These five can each exercise their one (1) vote and stop almost any action of that body. In most democracies, each person who meets certain basic requirements has one vote and it takes a majority to defeat or save a proposal. Why, in a body that is supposed to promote democracy, would five

(5!) nations, or 2.7% of the total, be given so much power? How can one expect other nations to take the body very seriously and to respect its decisions when it is obviously controlled by the five. That body is now more than 50 years old. Perhaps what worked in the past must be revisited in light of the emerging realities of today's global society.

The International Monetary Fund (IMF) - Heavily controlled by the United States of America and other developed countries, this bank disallows small nations' planned health care and education expenditures for citizens in favor of loan repayment and economic restructuring. The draconian control measures have caused national economies to collapse. When developing countries withdraw from IMF programs, we will begin to see the end of the IMF. When one nation dares to do the right thing for its citizens, others will follow. It takes the support of the many for any system or institution to stand. When many countries respond to systems without integrity by withdrawing their support, that system or institution will not stand. The IMF does not serve global advancement if its actions are controlled by the few to the detriment of the many or when its policies work against its clients—the developing nations. The 21st century will usher in new leadership of the IMF in the wake of the resignation of Michel Camdessus, its president of 12 years. That resignation is effective in February 2000. That new leadership must bring with it an appreciation of sovreignty and a respect for global good.

North Atlantic Treaty Organization (NATO)—Does anyone know why NATO took on Slobodan Milosevic in Yugoslavia in the Spring of 1999 with bombing attacks which were supposed to bring an end to his government's oppression of ethnic Albanians living there? Why was this issue not taken up by the United Nations? Why was that country decimated without an attempt at negotiation through the world body of nations? Some NATO member countries have admitted that their arms were twisted by the United States of America. At least one country indicated there were implied threats that if they voted against the bombing, their World Bank loans would not be approved for the next year. This takes us back to misuse of international financial assistance institutions. Why do we in the United States of America tolerate such bully mentality and actions on the part of our government? Do we have more fear than we have courage? Do we have to constantly remind others and ourselves of our supposed warrior superiority so that maybe someone will believe it, alone, makes *us* superior? Do we not trust more mental and spiritual approaches to conflict resolution?

United Nations Missions—The United States of America and its European allies have waged a bombing war on Iraq for months now. It started in December 1998, just as the House announced an impeachment vote against President Clinton. It intensified as the Senate debated. But this continuing bombing comes after the United Nations was forced to withdraw its Arms Inspection Team because Iraq proved that Team members from the United States of America were engaged in spy activity while in that country! What an embarrassment that must have been to the United Nations. Of course, the UN mission had to be abandoned. The Inspection Team had lost face and respect in the world community. Is this participation in a global society with integrity?

RESPONSIBILITY TO THE PEOPLE

It is understandable that appointed officials feel some responsibility to the people who appointed them. However, in their appointed positions they are expected to enforce laws and provisions put in place to serve *the people*. So, they are still the servants of the people. Because of that their ultimate responsibility is to listen to their own internal voice to assure their actions reflect that which is for the greater good of the people who are really picking up the tab for their salaries.

An excellent example of questionable integrity with the people of California is raised in the case of Ward Connerly, appointed in 1993 by California Governor Pete Wilson to the Board of Regents which governs the University of California (UC) system of 14 campuses around the state. Immediately after joining the Regents, Connerly initiated a fight against affirmative action admissions consideration for Hispanics, African Americans and Native Americans on all UC campuses. He prevailed. After bitter fights, a voter referendum and continued clashes and demonstrations on the campuses,[18] the debate still continues in California about whether abolishing affirmative action was in the best interests of the citizens of California.[19]

At last report, Connerly was working on two additional changes: the elimination of preferential admissions consideration for the children of alumni and major financial supporters; the second is the abolition of ethnic studies — all ethnic and women's studies programs on all campuses.

It should be noted that Connerly successfully argued in support of benefits for domestic partners in the University of California system. He reasoned that sexual preference should not determine eligibility for coverage.

CHAPTER 5:
Integrity In Leadership—
Military Officials

Military officials are out of the loop of this discussion on integrity, you might think, because of their separate rules for living and separate social structure. I maintain they are very much in the loop. They have a responsibility to all of us. After all, we send our children to them to become fodder in wars and other acts of violence. Military officials first have a responsibility to protect the lives of those who are in their charge and under their care. They also have a responsibility to exercise integrity in and maintain control over their relationships with others in the military-industrial complex. Some of the areas in which the military has not carried out this responsibility with integrity are as follows:

1. Development, testing and use of chemical and biological warfare (Acquired Immune Deficiency Syndrome or AIDS)
2. The testing of chemical weapons on its own military personnel
3. Use of land mines
4. Over-zealous disciplinary action, harassment and the scapegoating of trainees and others

DEVELOPMENT, TESTING AND USE OF CHEMICAL & BIOLOGICAL WEAPONS

The development and testing of chemical and biological weapons have created major dilemmas for this nation and others in the world. If the United States developed the AIDS virus in a Fort Dietrick (Aberdeen, Maryland) laboratory, as has been suggested,[20] and if it was spread world-wide via tainted vaccines we provided to the World Health Organization and possibly other aid organizations, as many believe, then this nation has caused the deaths of millions of children, and defenseless adults in developing countries. With whole countries being decimated, one can only ask, "Why?" And if we supply the rationale from our Western (Eurocentric) scientific training for why any experiment is done, we get, "For control." If this scenario is true, we are national and international outlaws and we will be hard-pressed to overcome the lack of integrity of this one deed. I would like to think the government did not develop the virus, but the following examples of known experiments leaves us unable to be sure.

In the early 1970s, we became aware of the Tuskegee Syphilis Experiment in which more than 400 African American male sharecroppers and day laborers in Alabama were subjects in a government study *designed* to explore the effects of untreated syphilis. These men were studied from 1932 to 1972 through their painful and debilitating lives until their deaths. This occured even though penicillin had been discovered to cure syphilis in the 1940s and could have been administered to the men as early as 1946. For the sake of understanding how syphilis ravaged the body, the treatment was withheld from these men.[21]

About the same time, we learned of other atrocities. Painful lobotomies were being performed on prisoners and inmates in state mental facilities without consent. These, too, were halted after public outcry.[22] Clandestine and unwanted sterilizations of teens and minorities in public clinics in the United States of America were also in the news in the 1970s. These are alluded to in a 1997 New York Times article on the Swedish sterilization scandal.[23] This excellent editorial calls on the Swedish government to set an example for other governments "confronted with evidence of undefensible behavior" by responding honestly to the allegations and generously to those harmed.

So, you can see why the possibility of more experimentation leads me to ask world military establishments to review the development, testing and use of biological and chemical weapons through the integrity lens and 7-Step Process offered in this book and to study the examples specific to these issues in Section II.

I am aware that the fact that people of color comprise 70% of the world population is not lost on northern hemispheric (non-colored) peoples. The fear of annihilation has driven this group too long. You can no longer be controlled by your fears. I am also aware that chemical and biological weapons are referred to as the "poor man's bomb," suggesting they are the weapon of choice for developing countries: cheap and effective.

You in developing countries must help stop the cycle of escalating violence. During World War II, 50% of casualties were among civilians. During the Cold War, civilian casualties have been rising to the point that in the 1990s, the most violent decade of the Cold War, unarmed civilians made up 90% of the casualties. Over 2,000,000 children have been killed in wars over the past 10 years. In a recently televised documentary, "Children of War" by Alan and Susan Raymond (HBO, Feb. 2000), the millions of children victimized by, involved in fighting and facing the ravages of war were finally seen and given a voice. Chemical and biological weapons do not selectively kill adults; they will wipe out the *next* generation — the world's children.

TESTING OF CHEMICAL & BIOLOGICAL WEAPONS ON OUR OWN PERSONNEL

On Sunday afternoons in the 1950's, one of the most popular television programs was "Victory At Sea." Each show featured some battle, encounter or operation from World War II that occurred at sea. The newsreel-like footage of planes and aircraft carriers, sailors, grand music and thrilling narration took on a note of horror in one very poignant program. I will never forget it. Sailors, scores of them, all in white, lined up like ducks in squatting positions on the deck of their aircraft carrier, were sprayed with chemical/biological agents by a plane that flew overhead. It was a test of these weapons using our own troops as the guinea pigs. The narrator heralded them for their bravery and dedication to their country. They were heroes. It is that kind of footage that leads me to believe the charges about Agent Orange and its use on our own ground troops in Viet Nam. These personnel were not asked to participate in testing. These personnel trusted their safety from agents produced for use against the "enemy." If the U.S. government violated that trust, it places our military officials outside the limits of integrity.

USE OF LAND MINES

The military-industrial establishment in the United States of America must have a major investment in land mines and receive tremendous profit from their sale. What else would explain the extreme resistance by this country to banning their use? In fact, by December 1997, 124 countries had signed the Ottawa Treaty. The Treaty bans the use, stockpiling, production and transfer of anti-personnel land mines. The United States of America has, so far, refused to sign. These mines are planted in 70 countries. I find that astounding. Each year, 26,000 civilians are killed or injured by the 100 million land mines that are planted in countries around the world. In Angola, land mines outnumber children; in Somalia, 75% of the land mine victims are children hurt while playing or walking in areas previously unexplored by these youth. For every mine cleared, there are 20 more planted.[24]

Land mines are indiscriminate about who they claim as victims and are too easily lost track of. They are not removed after their utility no longer exists. Our military leaders and we as citizens can use the two-part process for practicing integrity to look for options which will meet the needs of our government and the manufacturers who resist banning their use.

OVER-ZEALOUS DISCIPLINARY ACTION, HARASSMENT and SCAPEGOATING

When troops are disciplined and harm comes to them, sometimes we hear about it if the person dies. But, most times, these incidents do not see the light of day. They become the military's dirty secrets. We entrust our loved ones to military officials. Therefore, we encourage commanding officers, at all levels, to take steps to assure the safety of *all* their charges from their own action and that of others, including the peers of their charges.

More recently, women in the military are coming forward to tell of abuses against them by their comrades and commanding officers. In November 1996, the Air Force and Navy were planning to re-emphasize their zero-tolerance policy for sexual harassment in the wake of the problems which were being reported in the Army. Among the Army's cited problems were (1) the filing of criminal charges against two drill instructors and a captain accused of raping, sexually harassing and having improper contact with at least 12 young female recruits at a Maryland facility and(2) sexual charges against a drill sergeant and instructor at a Virginia facility.

A hotline was established in an effort to find others subjected to sexual harassment in the Maryland facility and more than 3,000 calls were received. Of those, 341 were deemed credible enough to turn over to investigators. Eighty-six of these complaints related to Aberdeen Ordinance Center (Maryland) and 255 others were related to other military sites.[25A] Such figures suggest the problem is widespread. These women are "paying for" someone else's "stuff" simply because they want to serve their country in traditionally male roles.

Recent disciplinary actions against military personnel for mistreatment of those under them include the non-judicial ruling (reduction in rank from general to colonel) of Air Force Brig. Gen. Robert T. Newell for sexual misconduct;[25B] and court martial of Sgt. Maj. Gene C. McKinney who was accused by six women, who do not know each other, of propositioning, grabbing or threatening them.[25C]

The July 1999 beating death of a young sailor, Barry Winchell, by his peers is believed to have been motivated by revelation that Winchell was gay.[26] It is hard to believe that no commander of any rank above those involved knew anything of the planned attack on this young man.

SECTION II:

ACHIEVING INTEGRITY
WITH PRACTICE

SECTION II:
Achieving Integrity with Practice

HOW TO USE THIS SECTION

The following pages have been developed as a resource or guide for the reader to the *practice of integrity*. As you confront one of the issues discussed in Section I or a related issue, consult this section of the book (Section II) for an example of how to utilize the 7-Step Process for Practicing Integrity.

The 7-Step Process is preceded by a statement of this writer's guiding principles for the issue. This *integrity position* is symbolized by **IP**. It gives the reader a brief rationale for the options presented in the example which follows. Each example is complete in itself. To obtain a fuller explanation of the *integrity position* found at the beginning of each chapter in Section II, look up the issue in the index and go to the page in Section I which explains this writer's rationale more fully.

Notwithstanding the completeness of each example (chapter) in Section II, the reader is encouraged to read the Introduction and Chapter 1 before attempting to use the 7-Step Process. Underlying concepts and assumptions are explained and the argument for the use of the 7-Step Process for Practicing Integrity is found in those places.

A practice form is provided for your use.

Practicing Integrity

Situation: _____

STEPS

1 RELAX	2 FORM QUESTIONS	3 TOOL	4A TOOL RESPONSE	4B BODY RESPONSE	5 OPTIONS	6A TOOL RESPONSE	6B BODY RESPONSE	7 DO IT

CHAPTER 6:
Owning Your Own Power

IP When you recognize and accept your power to make a new decision every moment of every day, you acknowledge your power to change any circumstance in your life. When you use that power to change your experience, you are owning your power — exercising your personal power — and practicing personal integrity. When you find yourself harboring unhealthy emotions or feeling negative in a particular situation, which is troublesome or uncomfortable, remember that you have the power to make the change to something better using the steps below.

Part 1: Knowing the right thing to do or not do

The first thing one has to do in the practice of integrity is know the right thing to do or not do. There are four steps in this part of the process:

Step 1:   Sit quietly and close your eyes. Take a few deep abdominal breaths. Drop the shoulders; loosen the jaw; relax.

Step 2:   Form your question(s) about the feeling, situation, or discomfort. For example, "Is any good coming of these emotions?" "Do I want to stay in this situation?" You may want to write down your questions.

Step 3:   **Visualize a traffic light.** Assign green to represent "Yes;" red is a definite "NO!"

Step 4:   **While visualizing the traffic light, ask each of the questions you formed in Step 2 and wait for your tool to give you your answer. You will also *feel* that the answer(s) is right.** Write down your answers.

Part II. How to do the right thing

This is the action-taking Part. Your goal is to find the easiest way for you to do the right thing.

Step 5:   **Think of all of your options for action to carry out the answer you received from Step 4 above.** Write down your options.

Step 6:   **Run each option through your mind as you visualize your tool. Observe the reaction of your traffic light. If you get a definitive, high quality answer, go on to Step 7. If you don't get a high quality, definitive yes for any option, give yourself more time to come up with additional options (Step 5) and take them back through Step 6.**

Step 7:   **Move on your right action. Remember that it's *your* answer and may not be the answer your spouse, parent, or friend would have gotten. Don't let others' opinions keep you from implementing your right action. Do it!**

    You will also *feel* this answer is right.

CHAPTER 7:
Living Your Life Purpose

IP When you have found your life purpose, you will feel a sense of peace and joy. That purpose may not be an easy road to walk, but you will feel good about it. As you try to find your life purpose, you will need to assess many opportunities that present themselves, suggestions from others and desires of your own. These steps may help.

Part 1: Knowing the right thing to do or not do

The first thing one has to do in the practice of integrity is know the right thing to do or not do. There are four steps in this part of the process:

Step 1:   Sit quietly. Take a few deep abdominal breaths. Drop the shoulders; loosen the jaw; relax.

Step 2:   Form your question(s) about what is right for you right now.

You might include such questions as:

1. Does this work bring me joy?

2. Is there something I would love to do but don't feel as if I can?

Step 3:   Visualize a big light bulb or one of the other tools mentioned in Chapter 1. The bulb lights when your answer is "Yes."

Step 4: While visualizing the tool you have selected, ask each of the questions you face about your life right now and wait for your tool to give you your answer. You will also *feel* that the answer is right.

Part II. How to do the right thing

This is the action-taking Part. Your goal is to find the easiest way for you to do the right thing.

Step 5: Think of all of your options for action to carry out the answer you received from Step 4 above.

For the purpose of this example, lets assume the answer to your first question was "No" and "Yes" to the second.

Options might look like the following:

1. I could learn new skills in my field, which I love, and seek greater challenge.
2. I could ask for more difficult work to help me develop my skills.
3. I could volunteer to teach disabled people this skill.

Or

1. I have always wanted my own business; I will talk to the bank about a loan.
2. I don't have the training to do that work, but I could volunteer at the local agency to start learning.
3. I am fascinated by that; but, I don't know if I can support myself if I quit my job and do it. I could research it and see.

Step 6: Run each option through your mind as you visualize your tool. Observe the reaction of your tool. If you get a definitive, high quality answer, go on to Step 7. If you don't get a high quality, definitive answer, give yourself more time to come up with additional options (Step 5) and take them back through Step 6.

Step 7: Move on your right action. Remember that it's *your* answer. Do it!

You will also *feel* this answer is right for you.

CHAPTER 8:
Speaking One's Mind

IP Whether or not we open our mouths and actually speak to the point, pick up pen and paper, write and mail that letter, or pick up the phone and actually make the call is the difference. Those actions are the difference between practicing integrity and merely *feeling* outrage, *recognizing* injustice, *feeling* empathy or anger. Not speaking out puts the individual in alliance with the wrong doers and those who are not practicing integrity.

Take the example of a household mover who arrives late. It is near darkness, the truck is too small, it has no lights and it is starting to rain on the boxes stacked in the courtyard ready to be moved to the new residence.

Part 1: Knowing the right thing to do or not do

The first thing one has to do in the practice of integrity is know the right thing to do or not do. There are four steps in this part of the process:

Step 1: Sit quietly. Take a few deep abdominal breaths. Drop the shoulders; loosen the jaw; relax.

Step 2: Form your questions about what is right.

Your questions might include:

1. Am I right to be outraged about the treatment from this moving company?

2. Should I express my outrage?

Step 3: **Visualize a traffic light, or a large clock. You may come up with another tool:**

Assign green to represent "Yes;" red is a definite "NO!" The louder the clock ticks, the closer you are to what's right for you.

Step 4: **While visualizing the tool you have selected, ask each of the questions you face and watch the reaction of your tool. You will also *feel* the answer is right.**

Part II. How to do the right thing

This is the action-taking Part. Your goal is to find the easiest way for you to do the right thing.

Step 5: **Think of all of your options for action to carry out the answer you received from Step 4 above.** For the purpose of this example, let's assume your clock ticked wildly when you asked both questions above. So you are now looking for the easiest way for YOU to express your outrage.

Your options might include:

1. Should I report that company to the Better Business Bureau to protect others from experiencing what I went through?

2. Should I talk to the owner and explain why I can't recommend him to others?

3. Should I tell my friend, who is considering the same company, about my experience?

4. Should I do all three of the above and file for damages through small claims court?

Step 6: **Run each option through your mind as you visualize your tool. Observe the reaction of your tool. If you get a definitive, high quality answer, go on to Step 7.**

If you don't get a high quality, definitive answer, give yourself more time to come up with additional options (Step 5) and take them back through Step 6.

Step 7:   Move on your right action. Remember that it's *your* answer and not the answer your spouse, parent, or friend might get. Do it!

You will also *feel* this answer is right for you.

CHAPTER 9:
Racism, Sexism and Other Prejudice

IP Our words, actions, thoughts cannot violate another's humanity —or person-hood — if you are practicing integrity. The essence of the practice of integrity is the ability to see oneself and everyone else as individual patterns in Life's wallpaper bin. You may not like a pattern for yourself, but the pattern is still a valid expression of divine artistry.

When faced with an emotion with which you are uncomfortable and you are not sure of the source of the discomfort, go through the following process.

Part 1: Knowing the right thing to do or not do

The first thing one has to do in the practice of integrity is know the right thing to do or not do. The source of discomfort is very important, but what is just as important is acknowledging, then *listening* to the Voice of discomfort and then looking for more appropriate actions. There are four steps in this part of the process:

Step 1: Sit quietly. Take a few deep abdominal breaths. Drop the shoulders; loosen the jaw; relax.

Step 2: **Form your question(s) about the source of discomfort so that you get "yes" or "no" answers.** For example, "Is the thought I just had/statement I just heard: 'I sure don't want to work for him!', racist?" Or ask yourself, "Did I move from my seat in the movie because a male couple came and sat next to me?"

Step 3: **Visualize a huge thermometer.** All of the bright red mercury is below the lines of gradation. The highest point on the thermometer represents "Yes." If the mercury stays in the bulb at the bottom, the answer is "No." You might also choose to use the traffic light.

Step 4: **While visualizing the tool you have selected, ask about the source of discomfort using the questions you formed in Step 2 and wait for your tool to give you your answer. You will also *feel* that the answer is right.**

Part II. How to do the right thing

This is the action-taking Part. The goal here is to find the easiest way for you to do the right thing. If one has accepted the premise presented here, that racist and sexist behavior, as well as behavior borne out of other forms of prejudice, is not the behavior appropriate for one practicing integrity, then one has to look for another way to be that *does* represent right action and in a way that is comfortable.

Step 5: **Think of all of your options for action to carry out the answer you received from Step 4 above.**

For example, your options might include:

1. I could welcome the new supervisor and keep an open mind.
2. I could ask others in the company to keep an open mind.
3. I could be sure I speak up and let the new supervisor know when I think something is a good idea and will work and when I don't.

Or

1. I could keep my current seat unless the couple's behavior is offensive to me.

2. I could recognize that someone might feel the same way about me and know that we are all connected anyway and keep my seat.

3. I could strike up a conversation with them and learn if they experience the movie differently from my own experience of it.

Step 6: **Run each option through your mind as you visualize your tool.** This time, the mercury in the bulb of the thermometer rises as the proposed actions move closer and closer to real integrity for you. **Observe the reaction of your tool. If you get a definitive, high quality answer, go on to Step 7. If you don't get a high quality, definitive answer, give yourself more time to come up with additional options (Step 5) and take them back through Step 6.**

Step 7: **Move on your right action. Do it!** Remember that it's *your* answer and may not be easy. However, you will also *feel* this answer is right.

CHAPTER 10:
Sexual Harassment

IP Sexual harassment is any UNWANTED attention to the sex of another person with whom we share the work environment or work related responsibilities. This includes but is not limited to comments, touch, pressure for sexual involvement by those in positions of power over the person, use of offensive images, and intense looks. To be in integrity is to respect the totality of the being of another and to respect the sensibilities of others.

Part 1: Knowing the right thing to do or not to do

The first thing one has to do in the practice of integrity is know the right thing to do or not to do. There are four steps in this part of the process:

Step 1:   **Sit quietly. Take a few deep abdominal breaths. Drop the shoulders; loosen the jaw; relax.**

Step 2:   **Form your question(s) about what is right.**

The questions might be as follows:

1. Although he said he has a girlfriend, should I give him this nude picture of myself?

2. Should I send this photo via Internet to this married man who is interested in me?

3. Although she tries to ignore me and cuts me off when I approach her, should I set a team lunch at my club and require her to meet me there?

4. Does inserting this pin-up photo in the manual constitute harassment of the two women who use the manual even though they know it's not meant to embarrass them?

Step 3: **Visualize a big light bulb**. The bulb lights when your answer is "Yes."

Step 4: **While visualizing the light bulb, ask each of the questions you formed at Step 2 and wait for your tool to give you your answer. You will also** *feel* **that the answer is right.**

Part II. How to do the right thing

There are three steps in this *second* part of the process for practicing integrity. This is the action-taking Part. The goal here is to find the easiest way to do the right thing.

Step 5: **Think of all of your options for action to carry out the answer you received from Step 4 above.**

Let's assume your bulb did not light on the question of giving your nude photo, sending your photo via the Internet and setting up a required lunch meeting for the object of your interest in space that is a part of your "turf" rather than in the office. Let's assume your bulb did light on question 4 regarding the manual which women use and the wisdom of inserting questionable material. The options may be few in such situations.

You might begin your options list with:

1. Leave the gentleman with a girlfriend alone after letting him know you are interested in him should something change in his availability.

2. Give the gentleman with a girlfriend your business card.

3. Send the gentleman with a girlfriend a humorous birthday card.

Or

1. Send the married gentleman the web address of a marriage counselor.

2. Send the married gentleman an Internet joke about infidelity.

3. Let the married gentleman know you are not willing to be No. 2.

Or

1. Arrange a non-lunch meeting in the office and stick to business to earn her respect.

2. Accept her non-interest at this time and re-direct your attentions.

3. Move yourself from her direct line of supervision to create more comfort for you both.

Or

1. Give the manual without the offensive material to the two women.

2. Recognize that the picture shows disrespect for the opposite sex and your wife and daughter are of the opposite sex and you would be embarrassed if they knew you were distributing such material and forgo inserting it in the manual.

3. Decide that there is a time and place for everything and the manual is not the time or place for this photo.

Step 6: **Run each option through your mind as you visualize a large ticking clock. The louder the ticking becomes the closer you are to your truth and the right action for you. Observe the reaction of your tool. If you get a definitive, high quality ticking, go on to Step 7. If you don't get a high quality, definitive answer, give yourself more time to come up with additional options (Step 5) and take them back through Step 6.**

Step 7: **Move on your right action. Remember that it's *your* answer. Do it!**

You will also *feel* this answer is right.

CHAPTER 11:
Taking Advantage of the Employer

IP To be in integrity with the public for *whom* you work, you as civil servants cannot misuse the resources with which you are entrusted. You recognize and understand that you are guardians of the public good and have a significant responsibility to use the time, money and other resources in the achievement of the mission of your agency.

Part 1: Knowing the right thing to do or not to do

The first thing one has to do in the practice of integrity is know the right thing to do or not to do. There are four steps in this part of the process:

Step 1: Sit quietly. Take a few deep abdominal breaths. Drop the shoulders; loosen the jaw; relax.

Step 2: Form your question(s) about what is right.

The questions might be similar to these:

1. I want to call my mother and see if my daughter's fever has broken. Should I?

2. No one will know I picked these receipts up off the floor and they are not really mine. Can I just go ahead and submit them and get back some of the money I've lost in the past?

3. My late date last night has left me fatigued. I think I will file today instead of working on draft policies. Is that an integrity problem?

Step 3:   **Visualize a big light bulb**. The bulb lights when your answer is "Yes."

Step 4:   **While visualizing the light bulb, ask each of the questions you formed at Step 2 and wait for your tool to give you your answer. You will also *feel* that the answer is right.**

Let's assume our bulb gives us a brilliant light (yes) for calling mother to check on our daughter and it stayed unlit on filing the bogus receipts. We also got a dimly lit bulb for filing rather than working on policies.

Part II. How to do the right thing

There are three steps in this *second* part of the process for practicing integrity. This is the action-taking Part. The goal here is to find the easiest way to do the right thing.

Step 5:   **Think of all of your options for action to carry out the answer you received from Step 4 above.**

You might begin your options list as follows:

1. Call mother at lunch time when everyone is out of the office and the calls are light. That way, no one I work with will be inconvenienced.

2. Call mother quickly, now, to ease my mind and see if I need to call the doctor.

Or

1. I can toss the receipts and know I will receive what's due to me.

2. I can toss the receipts and talk to my accounting department about how to get reimbursed for underpayment of expenses in the past.

3. I can request a credit card for business charges and eliminate the numerous cash payments I make that never get reimbursed.

Or

Since the bulb only lit dimly, regarding the filing rather than working on the more demanding tasks, you need to explore the reasons for the dim light and try to propose refinements that will move it to a bright light. So, our options might be:

1. Before deciding to file, review the deadlines for the policies, the status and whether taking the day will adversely affect the deadline.

2. File for the morning until getting more energy after a power nap at lunch and then move to the policy work.

Step 6:   **Run each option through your mind as you visualize a large light bulb. Observe the reaction of your tool. If you get a definitive, high quality light, go on to Step 7. If you don't get a high quality, definitive answer, give yourself more time to come up with additional options (Step 5) and take them back through Step 6.**

Step 7:   **Move on your right action. Remember that it's *your* answer. Do it!**

You will also *feel* this answer is right.

CHAPTER 12:
Playing Favorites in Funding

IP To maintain integrity with the public, funding decisions must be based on the outcome of the review process and the goals of the funding program. To use the funds to achieve other goals, especially personal goals, is misuse of funds.

Part 1: Knowing the right thing to do or not to do

The first thing one has to do in the practice of integrity is know the right thing to do or not to do. There are four steps in this part of the process:

Step 1: **Sit quietly. Take a few deep abdominal breaths. Drop the shoulders; loosen the jaw; relax.**

Step 2: **Form your question(s) about what is right.**

The questions might be similar to these:

1. Organization A submitted a proposal in a category which is not its strength, but they do good work; I would like to fund this proposal although they are not the best in this area. Should I?

2. My former deputy has just gone to Organization B. This grant will help them continue his program and boost his future with the organization. The grant scored high but in a category with

little money and we can't reach this organization if we do it strictly by rank.

Step 3:   **Visualize a big thermometer with all of the mercury in the bottom.** The mercury rises to the top of the tube when your answer is "Yes."

Step 4:   **While visualizing the thermometer, ask each of the questions you formed at Step 2 and wait for your tool to give you your answer. You will also** *feel* **that the answer is right.**

Part II. How to do the right thing

There are three steps in this *second* part of the process for practicing integrity. This is the action-taking Part. The goal here is to find the easiest way to do the right thing.

Step 5:   **Think of all of your options for action to carry out the answer you received from Step 4 above.**

If you got mercury spurting out of the thermometer at question 1, you might look for options that help you determine how to fund the subject grant. If you received no reaction from your thermometer when asking the question about your former deputy's organization, the position of integrity would be not to fund it — at least from your announced funds.

You might begin your options list as follows:

1. Recognize that Organization A has the likelihood of developing excellent capabilities in the area where they have applied and provide capacity building funds to make the grant instead of the announced funds or establish a portion of those funds for capacity building grants.

2. Make a one-year grant instead of a multi-year grant to limit the demand on the available funds.

3. Fund a limited aspect of the proposed program that will allow the capacity building.

Or

1. Identify other sources of funding that the former deputy's organization can be encouraged to pursue.

2. Encourage re-applying at the next funding cycle.

3. Call a sister agency and tell them about Organization B's proposal which fits their primary interests and encourage contact/funding.

Step 6:   Run each option through your mind as you visualize a large thermometer.

The higher the mercury rises the closer you are to your truth and the right action for you. Observe the reaction of your tool. If you get a definitive, high quality rise in the mercury, go on to Step 7. If you don't get a high quality, definitive answer, give yourself more time to come up with additional options (Step 5) and take them back through Step 6.

Step 7:   Move on your right action. Remember that it's *your* answer. Do it!

You will also *feel* this answer is right.

CHAPTER 13:
De-Emphasizing The Truth

IP De-emphasizing the truth is misrepresenting the truth. Depending on the circumstances, playing with the truth can endanger large numbers of individuals and represent a mis-use of the taxpayers' dollars when government is involved. Taxpayers expect the government to protect them.

Part 1: Knowing the right thing to do or not to do

The first thing one has to do in the practice of integrity is know the right thing to do or not to do. There are four steps in this part of the process:

Step 1: **Sit quietly. Take a few deep abdominal breaths. Drop the shoulders; loosen the jaw; relax.**

Step 2: **Form your question(s) about what is right.**

For agency representatives, ask

1. Does the report accurately portray the conditions as nearly as I can tell?

2. Is this a balanced report? That is, does any area of the report overstate or stress the negative without giving the positives which offset the negatives and vice versa?

3.   Will this report mislead authorities in this agency? Will it mislead people in the public?

Step 3:   **Visualize a traffic light.**   Assign green to represent "Yes;" red is a definite "NO!"

Step 4:   **While visualizing the traffic light, ask each of the questions you formed at Step 2 and wait for your tool to give you your answer. You will also *feel* that the answer is right.**

Part II. How to do the right thing

There are three steps in this *second* part of the process for practicing integrity. This is the action-taking Part. The goal here is to find the easiest way to do the right thing.

Step 5:   **Think of all of your options for action to carry out the answer you received from Step 4 above.**

We can assume that the traffic light gave you a green signal on the first question. It gave you a green light, or "yes" answer for the report being balanced. So, you have a good report. You also got a red light for the third question on the reports potential for misleading readers. How do you practice integrity with its alarming contents?

Your list of options might look like this:

1.   Propose to supervisors a plan for releasing findings along with a plan to fix the problem. The problem then becomes a moot point and the agency is a hero.

2.   Let the supervisor make the decision regarding taking the report as submitted or requesting changes.

3.   Suggest calling a news conference. Report the problem. Indicate the difficulty with repairing or curing the problem. Indicate need for public support and input. Announce a public meeting.

Step 6:   **Run each option through your mind as you visualize your traffic light. Observe the reaction of your tool. If you get a definitive, high quality green light, go on to**

Step 7. If you don't get a high quality, definitive answer, give yourself more time to come up with additional options (Step 5) and take them back through Step 6.

Step 7:   Move on your right action. Remember that it's *your* answer. Do it!

You will also *feel* this answer is right.

CHAPTER 14:
Whistle Blowing

IP One who decides to "blow the whistle" — a term used to describe the release of damaging information without authorization — is usually exposing some secret which puts the agency or department in a less than favorable light. Exposure to light may cause a halt to that practice. That is, at the least, what the whistle blower hopes for. People who take this route are usually anguished and torn by the call to practice integrity. Before deciding if this is the best course of action for you, consider the two-part process below for the practice of integrity to explore other options.

Part 1: Knowing the right thing to do or not do

The first thing one has to do in the practice of integrity is know the right thing to do or not do. There are four steps in this part of the process:

Step 1:   Sit quietly. Take a few deep abdominal breaths. Drop the shoulders; loosen the jaw; relax.

Step 2:   Form your question(s) about the company practice or policy that concerns you.

For example:

1.   Can this practice really hurt people?

2.   Can this policy or practice be changed without doing even more harm?

3.   Can I live with myself if I continue to support this policy/practice with my silence?

Step 3:   Visualize one of the following tools:

> **a.   A traffic light.** Assign green to represent "Yes;" red is a definite "NO!"
>
> **b.   A huge thermometer.** All of the bright red mercury is below the lines of gradation. The highest point on the thermometer represents the right action for you.
>
> **c.   A big light bulb**. The bulb lights when your answer is "Yes."
>
> **d.   A large clock.** The ticking of the clock becomes louder and louder as you move closer to the right action for you. The ticking is loudest when you have reached the answer which represents your truth.

Step 4:   While visualizing the tool, ask each of the questions you face in your particular dilemma and wait for your tool to give you your answer. You will also *feel* that the answer is right.

Part II. How to do the right thing

There are three steps in this *second* part of the process for practicing integrity. This is the action-taking Part. The goal here is to find the easiest way for you to do the right thing.

Let's assume that your tool gave you a resounding "Yes!" to the first question of whether or not the practice could harm people and a less bright, but still a definite "Yes" to the second question of the possibility of changing the practice without causing more harm. Let's also assume that before you could complete asking the third question relating to living with yourself if you remained silent, you experienced the onset of a major headache. Your body is responding before the tool does and you are fortunate that your body is responding so clearly. That is the kind of body response you are looking for at the same time you observe the action of your tool. You now know that you cannot remain silent.

Step 5:   Think of all of your options for action to carry out the answer you received from Step 4 above. Write them down. You know that people can or are already being hurt by the particular practice and you also know that your tool suggests that some harm could come from changing the practice. It is important to consider what that harmful impact might be and consider ameliorating such impact as you develop options for your own action.

Your list of options might include the following:

1.   Consider what harm could come from changing the hurtful practice (e.g., smaller companies unable to afford changing to the new technology could lose contracts) and contact those actors and seek their suggestions for how to change the practice in a way that they are not unduly affected.

2. .   Since no boss likes to be presented with a problem without a solution, present the problem and a realistic solution to your supervisor with letters of support from those who will be affected. Offer to work with others to develop a cost estimate. Be prepared to take responsibility for next steps.

3.   Send E-mail messages to other concerned individuals, your supervisor, and his/her supervisor and request an opportunity to discuss alternatives to the existing practice before going to the press.

4.   "Leak" incriminating documents to the press.

Step 6:   Run each option through your mind as you visualize a large ticking clock. The ticking of the clock becomes louder and louder as you move closer to the right action for you. The ticking is loudest when you have reached the answer which represents your truth. Observe the reaction of your tool. If you get a definitive, high quality answer, go on to Step 7. If you don't get a high quality, definitive answer, give yourself more time to come up with additional options (Step 5) and take them back through Step 6.

Step 7. **Move on your right action. Remember that it's *your* answer. Do it!**

You will also *feel* this answer is right.

CHAPTER 15:
Promotions and Awards

IP Develop a guideline for when an award is given and when a promotion is given. Let your staff know what those requirements are and what the difference is between the two. Do not confuse this guideline with the guidelines set out by the agency for each award. Use these "rules" to help you, the deciding official, to make decisions about each promotion/award. Where promotions are frozen or there is no higher grade approved for a particular job title in your office, you have to decide if you are misusing the award system if you give awards in lieu of promotions. This, of course, is a different integrity issue.

Part 1: Knowing the right thing to do or not to do.

The first thing one has to do in the practice of integrity is know the right thing to do or not to do. There are four steps in this part of the process:

Step 1:   **Sit quietly. Take a few deep abdominal breaths. Drop the shoulders; loosen the jaw; relax.**

Step 2:   **Form your question(s) about what is right.**

The questions might be similar to the following:

1.   Is it prejudicial to give a promotion to Sally, who is a joy to work with, and an award to Janice, who is very confrontational, even though they worked miracles together on the same project?

2.   Is it fair to give Sally the promotion because she did most of the work on this project and give Janice an award even though she was the project manager?

Step 3:   **Visualize a big light bulb**. The bulb lights when your answer is "Yes."

Step 4:   **While visualizing the light bulb, ask each of the questions you formed at Step 2 and wait for your tool to give you your answer. You will also *feel* that the answer is right.**

Part II. How to do the right thing

There are three steps in this *second* part of the process for practicing integrity. This is the action-taking Part. The goal here is to find the easiest way to do the right thing.

Step 5:   **Think of all of your options for action to carry out the answer you received from Step 4 above.**

You might begin your options list with the following:

1.   Call the two employees in one at a time and discuss with them the choices you have and your desire to reward them both and see what they say.

2.   Ask Janice if she feels Sally's work merits a promotion or an award (based on the guidelines for the office) and ask her to write up her recommendation. Ask Sally to do the same regarding Janice.

Step 6:   **Run each option through your mind as you visualize a large ticking clock. The louder the ticking becomes the closer you are to your truth and the right action for you. Observe the reaction of your tool. If you get a definitive, high quality ticking, go on to Step 7. If**

you don't get a high quality, definitive answer, give yourself more time to come up with additional options (Step 5) and take them back through Step 6.

Step 7:   Move on your right action. Remember that it's *your* answer. Do it!

You will also *feel* this answer is right.

CHAPTER 16:
Animosity Between Branches
of Government

IP Actions taken by members of governmental systems are known around the world in a matter of minutes. Nothing we do can or will be kept out of the eye of the world public. If we value the structure of our government and believe in the institutions of the executive branch, legislative branch, and judicial branch, we are bound to exercise our responsibilities in a way that those *structures* are not diminished. It is their symbol of strength and presumption of national support which give them their power.

Part 1: Knowing the right thing to do or not to do

The first thing one has to do in the practice of integrity is know the right thing to do or not to do. There are four steps in this part of the process:

Step 1: Sit quietly. Take a few deep abdominal breaths. Drop the shoulders; loosen the jaw; relax.

Step 2: Form your question(s) about what is right.

The questions might be similar to the following:

1. Does this action promote and support the concept of the Congress and its role?

2.   Does this action bolster the trust of the public in the Congress/House/Senate/Presidency/Supreme Court?

3.   Does this action enhance the image of the U.S. Presidency in the world?

4.   Does this action support the responsibility of the President to conduct national business with other world leaders on a level playing field?

5.   Does this action truly serve the good of the country?

Step 3:   **Visualize a big light bulb**. The bulb lights when your answer is "Yes."

Step 4:   **While visualizing the light bulb, ask each of the questions you formed at Step 2 and wait for your tool to give you your answer. You will also *feel* that the answer is right.**

Part II. How to do the right thing

There are three steps in this *second* part of the process for practicing integrity. This is the action-taking Part. The goal here is to find the easiest way to do the right thing.

Step 5:   **Think of all of your options for action to carry out the answer you received from Step 4 above.**

Let's assume that after all is said and done, at question #5, you got a resounding dead light bulb. No, the action is not in the interest of the country. Now what to do is your question.

You might begin your options list:

1.   Leave my party affiliation out of the equation and vote my heart regardless of what others do.

2.   Discuss with colleagues the harm to the institution of Congress of:

-    Constantly fighting with the White House

-    Sensationalizing everything

-    Abdicating our role: turning *our* decision making role over to the people

-       Being late on the real important work of the Congress

    Try to get colleagues to reconsider the *way* we are conducting our business.

3.   Try to get colleagues to consider the harm to the institution of the Presidency when the incumbent:

-       Is crippled at a time when world economic crisis needs focus and leadership

-       Can't speak with authority on trade, treaty, terrorism if seen as embattled (weakened and without support) at home

-       Is seen as weaker because of presumed pre-occupation

-       May be tempted to make rash decisions to deflect attention, harming the country in world view

4.   Offer colleagues creative ways to do the work of House and Senate committees more efficiently.

5.   Threaten to leak damaging information if behavior is not halted.

6.   Leak damaging information so that the public understands there are no saints and things are not what they should be in the Capitol.

7.   Remind colleagues that we lead individually and as a nation only as long as the people here and world-wide support that notion. Use the Soviet Union's crash in three days as an example.

Step 6:   Run each option through your mind as you visualize a large ticking clock. The louder the ticking becomes the closer you are to your truth and the right action for you. Observe the reaction of your tool. If you get a definitive, high quality ticking, go on to Step 7. If you don't get a high quality, definitive answer, give yourself more time to come up with additional options (Step 5) and take them back through Step 6.

Step 7: **Move on your right action. Remember that it's *your* answer. Do it!**

You will also *feel* this answer is right.

CHAPTER 17:
Unbridled Partisanship &
Use Of Smoke Screens

IP Though elected with the help of party leaders and funds, the first responsibility of an elected official is the right and good representation of those who voted for that person. Sensationalizing matters grabs headlines while relegating to back pages more important decisions (e.g., budget decisions). This often occurs along party lines. Such use of smoke screens is an everyday tactic. In the practice of integrity, the party is third behind one's own heart and the people.

Part 1: Knowing the right thing to do or not to do.

The first thing one has to do in the practice of integrity is know the right thing to do or not to do. There are four steps in this part of the process:

Step 1: Sit quietly. Take a few deep abdominal breaths. Drop the shoulders; loosen the jaw; relax.

Step 2: Form your question(s) about what is right.

For example, your question might be:

Is this action good for the people?

Step 3:   **Visualize** a **traffic light**. Assign green to represent "Yes;" red is a definite "NO!"

Step 4:   **While visualizing the tool you have selected, ask each of the questions you face such as the questions in the example at Step 2 and wait for your tool to give you your answer. You will also** *feel* **that the answer is right.**

Part II. How to do the right thing

There are three steps in this *second* part of the process for practicing integrity. This is the action-taking Part. The goal here is to find the easiest way for you to do the right thing.

Step 5:   **Think of all of your options for action to carry out the answer you received from Step 4 above.**

If your traffic light is showing a brilliant red in response to the question asked in Step 4 above, there is cause for pause.

Your options list for practicing integrity might begin with:

1.   Don't participate in/vote for this action without getting an explanation that moves the traffic light from red to green.

2.   Offer another action that serves the people better, stressing the responsibility to place the people over the party.

3.   Express the opinion that the action is party-motivated without good intention and explain that I have something else to do for my constituents at that time and therefore, will not participate or vote.

4.   Vote against the measure.

Step 6:   **Run each option in Step 5 through your mind as you visualize your traffic light. Observe the reaction of your tool. If you get a definitive, high quality green, go on to Step 7. If you don't get a high quality, definitive answer, give yourself more time to come up with additional options (Step 5) and take them back through Step 6.**

Step 7:   **Move on your right action. Remember that it's** *your* **answer. Do it!**

You will also *feel* this answer is right.

CHAPTER 18:
Selling the Vote

IP You elected officials and your staffs have to listen to the lobbyists who are citizens, too, of the corporate and special interest type. In a democracy, these corporate and special interest voices are just as legitimate as the voices of individual citizens – but they are not *more* legitimate than the voices of individuals. The difference between the two is that corporate and special interest voices are reinforced with a big check. Those of us private citizens who send big checks get special recognition — our causes are considered, too. But what about the hundreds of thousands who sent small contributions, or more likely, no funds at all to support your campaign. If you are selling your vote to the highest bidder, we can neither get our fair share of your attention which is guaranteed by our citizenship nor can we be assured you will act in our best interest.

Part 1: Knowing the right thing to do or not to do

The first thing one has to do in the practice of integrity is know the right thing to do or not to do. There are four steps in this part of the process:

Step 1:   Sit quietly. Take a few deep abdominal breaths. Drop the shoulders; loosen the jaw; relax.

Step 2:   Form your question(s) about what is right.

For example, before accepting a contribution you might ask,

1.   "Does this business support my constituents' interests *and* work in their best interest (i.e., health, mental health, and economic well-being)?"

2.   "Would a majority of my constituents be happy to know I took this contribution?"

Step 3:   Visualize a traffic light. Assign green to represent "Yes;" red is a definite "NO!"

Step 4:   While visualizing your traffic light, ask each of the questions you formed at Step 2 and wait for your tool to give you your answer. You will also *feel* that the answer is right.

Part II. How to do the right thing

There are three steps in this *second* part of the process for practicing integrity. This is the action-taking Part. The goal here is to find the easiest way for you to do the right thing.

Step 5:   Think of all of your options for action to carry out the answer you received from Step 4. above.

Let's suppose your traffic light was decidedly red in response to question 2 in Step 2 above. You are looking for options for what to do to remain in integrity.

Your options list might include:

1.   I could decline the money.

2.   I could suggest it be given to the national party organization.

3.   I could encourage the contribution to an appropriate organization within my district.

Step 6:   Run each option through your mind as you visualize your traffic light. Observe the reaction of your tool. If you get a definitive, high quality green light, go on to Step 7. If you don't get a high quality, definitive answer, give yourself more time to come up with addi-

tional options (Step 5) and take them back through Step 6.

Step 7:   **Move on your right action. Remember that it's *your* answer. Do it!**

You will also *feel* this answer is right.

CHAPTER 19:
Wasting Money/Pork Barrels

IP While placed in the section for elected officials, this problem is encountered throughout the system of government in the United States of America — in every branch, in every department. Integrity in this area is discussed for government workers in all of these places whether elected, appointed or career civil servants. You have been brought to these positions with the full expectation that you will be good trustees of the people's money.

Part 1: Knowing the right thing to do or not to do

The first thing one has to do in the practice of integrity is know the right thing to do or not to do. There are four steps in this part of the process:

Step 1: **Sit quietly. Take a few deep abdominal breaths. Drop the shoulders; loosen the jaw; relax.**

Step 2: **Form your question(s) about what is right in this area.**

In your specific position, your level of concern may lead you to ask the following question:

1. Is money being wasted under my umbrella of responsibility that could be better used?

Step 3:   **Visualize a traffic light.** Assign green to represent "Yes;" red is a definite "NO!"

Step 4:   **While visualizing the traffic light, ask each of the questions you formed at Step 2 and wait for your tool to give you your answer. You will also** *feel* **that the answer is right.**

Part II. How to do the right thing

There are three steps in this *second* part of the process for practicing integrity. This is the action-taking Part. The goal here is to find the easiest way for you to do the right thing.

Step 5:   **Think of all of your options for action to carry out the answer you received from Step 4 above.**

Assuming a "Yes" answer, you may need more information. Your options will be different depending on your position.

Some of your options might include the following:

1.   Determine if money is dumped in the last quarter of the year to assure a larger budget in the next year.

2.   Determine if money is being spent lavishly in the first half of the year to assure there' no money left at the end of the year.

3.   Before voting for budget line items, ask, "Is there a pork barrel here?"

5.   Before voting, find out, "What's being cut to support the pork?" (Make a list of what I find and ask which things serve more people? What group needs the resources most? What promises are being broken?)

6.   Do something to reward the return of money at the end of the year.

7.   Do something to change the mind set that there is an endless stream of money for special prosecutors, pork barrel projects, etc.

8.   Do something to inspire project managers to come in on budget.

Step 6:   Run each option through your mind as you visualize a large ticking clock. Observe the reaction of your clock. If you get a definitive, high quality ticking clock, go on to Step 7. If you don't get a high quality, definitive answer, give yourself more time to come up with additional options (Step 5) and take them back through Step 6.

Step 7:   Move on your right action. Remember that it's *your* answer. Do it!

You will also *feel* this answer is right.

CHAPTER 20:
Lopsided Treaties and Trade Agreements

IP If it's lopsided, it automatically lacks integrity. Those of you who represent this country in such matters will be most suited to the work that needs to be done here. However, the general public can assist you by letting you know of our preference for integrity in our international agreements.

Part 1: Knowing the right thing to do or not to do

The first thing one has to do in the practice of integrity is know the right thing to do or not to do. There are four steps in this part of the process:

Step 1: **Sit quietly. Take a few deep abdominal breaths. Drop the shoulders; loosen the jaw; relax.**

Step 2: **Form your question(s) about what is right to do in this international arena.**

For example, those who work with international agreements, including agreements with Native American tribes, might list the goals for our own participation in such an agreement and then ask questions such as:

1. "Will we achieve our goals if we sign this agreement?"

2. "Is this agreement fair to all proposed signers?"

Step 3:   **Visualize a big light bulb.** The bulb lights when your answer is "Yes."

Step 4:   **While visualizing the light bulb, ask each of the questions you formed at Step 2 and wait for your tool to give you your answer. You will also *feel* that the answer is right.**

Part II. How to do the right thing

There are three steps in this *second* part of the process for practicing integrity. This is the action-taking Part. The goal here is to find the easiest way for you to do the right thing.

Step 5:   **Think of all of your options for action to carry out the answer you received from Step 4 above.**

Let's assume you have found you cannot achieve your goals if you sign the current agreement and that the bulb did not light on the question of fairness.

Your options might include:

1. Sitting with paper and pen and closed eyes. Relax (as in Step I, Part I) and ask, "How can I make this agreement more fair *and* achieve my goals?"

Representatives of other countries might get a list that looks like this:

A. Increase the price of my goods

B. Ration the amount of my goods I send to the U.S.A.

C. Create other markets

Representatives of the U.S.A. might get:

A. Phase in the tariffs

B. Reduce the amount of tariffs

C. Establish a review clause for reevaluation of success by all signors in three years. Incorporate a process for bringing swift remedy to those parties not fairly treated.

Step 6:   Run each option through your mind as you visualize your light bulb. Observe the reaction of your tool. If you get a definitive, high quality light, go on to Step 7. If you don't get a high quality, definitive answer, give yourself more time to come up with additional options (Step 5) and take them back through Step 6.

Step 7.   Move on your right action. Remember that it's *your* answer. Do it!

You will also *feel* this answer is right.

CHAPTER 21:
Misuse Of and Disrespect For International Organizations

"The world public has become disenchanted with both the political and financial leadership, which it no longer trusts to solve the problems of historical crises. Furthermore, all the individuals of humanity are looking for the answer to what the little individual can do that can't be done by great nations and great enterprises."

—R. Buckminster Fuller

IP The leaders of the world must regain their public's trust and belief in their ability to resolve historical crises. Leaders might start with leveling the playing field of international organizations to make them more representative. Withdrawing the special status and control given to some is mandatory. Achieving objectivity in international banking institutions is requisite. This can be done through efforts to truly understand and support the growth and development goals of their customers, create policy which supports that growth and development and eliminate the heavy influence of donor countries. If these institutions do not exist for the benefit of the customers, then they *should* not exist at all.

Part 1: Knowing the right thing to do or not to do

The first thing one has to do in the practice of integrity is know the right thing to do or not to do. There are four steps in this part of the process:

Step 1: Sit quietly. Take a few deep abdominal breaths. Drop the shoulders; loosen the jaw; relax.

Step 2: Form your question(s) about what is right.

The questions might include:

1. Should I use our veto power to keep the organization from discussing this subject since my country's role in the affair was less than honorable?

2. Should I pressure the Bank to cut next year's payments to Country Y since it did not support us in our military action against Country W?

Step 3: Visualize a big light bulb. The bulb lights when your answer is "Yes."

Step 4: While visualizing the light bulb, ask each of the questions you formed at Step 2 and wait for your tool to give you your answer. You will also *feel* that the answer is right.

Part II. How to do the right thing

There are three steps in this *second* part of the process for practicing integrity. This is the action-taking Part. The goal here is to find the easiest way to do the right thing.

Step 5: Think of all of your options for action to carry out the answer you received from Step 4. above.

Let's assume the answer you got to both questions was "No." Then you are looking for acceptable options to those proposed at Step 2.

You might begin your options list as follows:

1. I could ask for a limit to the depth of discussion/investigation to protect national security information.

2.   I could swallow our national pride and admit we made a mistake.

3.   I could acknowledge our over-reaction, apologize to the country we harmed and offer to compensate the victims.

Or

1.   We could continue to make contributions to the Bank with no strings attached and count on the good we do to win us friends.

2.   We could discontinue our contributions to the Bank until all nations sign an accord acknowledging the sovereignty of the bank and its decision-making procedures and lead the world nations in signing the accord.

Step 6:   **Run each option through your mind as you visualize a large ticking clock. The louder the ticking becomes the closer you are to your truth and the right action for you. Observe the reaction of your tool. If you get a definitive, high quality ticking, go on to Step 7. If you don't get a high quality, definitive answer, give yourself more time to come up with additional options (Step 5) and take them back through Step 6.**

Step 7:   **Move on your right action. Remember that it's *your* answer. Do it!**

You will also *feel* this answer is right.

CHAPTER 22:
Responsibility to the People

IP Indirectly but, very importantly, appointed officials have a responsibility to all the people in the jurisdiction over which they preside. You are bound to administer the laws in your mandate faithfully and in the best interest of the people. Even so, it is good to remember that you will never please all of the people all of the time.

Part 1: Knowing the right thing to do or not to do

The first thing one has to do in the practice of integrity is know the right thing to do or not to do. There are four steps in this part of the process:

Step 1: Sit quietly. Take a few deep abdominal breaths. Drop the shoulders; loosen the jaw; relax.

Step 2: Form your question(s) about what is right.

You might ask:

1. Does this action serve the largest number of the people I am appointed to serve? This question is not a superficial one. The answer may seem obvious if interest groups are easy to identify. But don't answer the question without going through the next two Steps.

Step 3:   **Visualize a huge thermometer.** All of the bright red mercury is below the lines of gradation. The highest point on the thermometer represents the right action for you.

Step 4:   **While visualizing the thermometer, ask each of the questions you formed at Step 2 and wait for your tool to give you your answer. You will also *feel* that the answer is right.**

Part II. How to do the right thing

There are three steps in this *second* part of the process for practicing integrity. This is the action-taking Part. The goal here is to find the easiest way for you to do the right thing.

Step 5:   **Think of all of your options for action to carry out the answer you received from Step 4 above.**

If the mercury in your thermometer did not go very far up the shaft, then you are looking for options to the proposed action; or you are looking for ways to modify the proposed action to make it good for the largest possible number of those you serve. You might sit quietly with pen and paper and ask:

"Is there another action that would serve the people better and accomplish the same thing?" Record everything that comes up.

Your list of options might include:

1. Reviewing the history of the issue to determine the roots of the mandate. That is, why it was instituted and what it was to accomplish; then looking at objective data on the outcomes to date and determining whether the objectives were attained and if not, why not. If objectives were not accomplished, try to determine how to address the reasons why the mandate failed to produce the desired results and create approaches to accomplish the objectives which focus on correcting the barriers.

2. Where you believe the mandate is no longer necessary engage people on both sides of the argument who are respected for their clear thinking, ability to connect to the public and feel its

pulse. Research the outcomes, difficulties and costs. Make a decision and provide a clear rationale.

3. Where the issue is bigger than the people you serve, sometimes you will be called upon to make the decision which moves humanity forward. When you go through Step 6, the appropriateness of this action will become very clear. In your heart of hearts you will know the right thing to do.

Step 6:   **Run each option through your mind as you visualize your thermometer. Observe the reaction of your tool. If you get a definitive, high quality rise in the mercury, go on to Step 7. If you don't get a high quality, definitive answer, give yourself more time to come up with additional options (Step 5) and take them back through Step 6.**

Step 7:   **Move on your right action. Remember that it's _your_ answer. Do it!**

You will also _feel_ this answer is right.

CHAPTER 23:
Development, Testing And
Use of Chemical & Biological Weapons

IP *If* chemical and biological weapons (CB/W) are required for an effective defense, the goal for their development and testing could be that testing not be done on human subjects. We also might become committed to development of CB/W with short-term impact and to development and promulgation of rules for their usage similar to the Geneva Accord.

Part 1: Knowing the right thing to do or not to do.

The first thing one has to do in the practice of integrity is know the right thing to do or not to do. There are four steps in this part of the process:

Step 1: Sit quietly. Take a few deep abdominal breaths. Drop the shoulders; loosen the jaw; relax.

Step 2: Form your question(s) about what is right

Your questions might be similar to the following:

1. Does this proposed CB/W have catastrophic long-term effects?

2. Will the testing of this CB/W affect the well-being of humans?

3. Is the use of this CB/W defensible based on the "Accord?"

Step 3:   **Visualize** a **traffic light**. Assign green to represent "Yes;" red is a definite "NO!"

Step 4:   **While visualizing the traffic light, ask each of the questions you formed at Step 2 and wait for your tool to give you your answer. You will also** *feel* **that the answer is right.**

Part II. How to do the right thing

There are three steps in this *second* part of the process for practicing integrity. This is the action-taking Part. The goal here is to find the easiest way for you to do the right thing.

Step 5:   **Think of all of your options for action to carry out the answer you received from Step 4. above.**

If your traffic light gave you only red lights, or more red lights than you feel comfortable with, you are looking for options.

You might list options such as:

1. Prevent further development until testing can be done without harm to humans.

2. Look for better ways to achieve the same military objective.

3. Look for other uses for these scientists.

4. Look for ways to convert this sophisticated array of equipment and facilities to life affirming uses.

Step 6:   **Run each option through your mind as you visualize the traffic light. Observe the reaction of your tool. If you get a definitive, high quality green light, go on to Step 7. If you don't get a high quality, definitive green light, give yourself more time to come up with additional options (Step 5) and take them back through Step 6.**

Step 7:   **Move on your right action. Remember that it's** *your* **answer. Do it!**

You will also *feel* this answer is right.

CHAPTER 24:
Testing of Chemical & Biological Weapons on Our Own Personnel

IP Most people in the military expect their lives will not be endangered for scientific purposes. They did not sign up to serve their country in that way. You are bound to respect the covenant between you and them and not endanger their health, their lives or the lives of their future generations without their completely informed consent.

Part 1: Knowing the right thing to do or not to do

The first thing one has to do in the practice of integrity is know the right thing to do or not to do. There are four steps in this part of the process:

Step 1:   Sit quietly. Take a few deep abdominal breaths. Drop the shoulders; loosen the jaw; relax.

Step 2:   Form your question(s) about what is right.

You may be conflicted by different positions being taken around you.

Ask your Inner Voice,

1. Will our own personnel be harmed by this action?

Step 3:   **Visualize a big light bulb**. The bulb lights when your answer is "Yes."

Step 4:   **While visualizing the light bulb, ask each of the questions you formed at Step 2 and wait for your tool to give you your answer. You will also *feel* that the answer is right.**

Part II. How to do the right thing

There are three steps in this *second* part of the process for practicing integrity. This is the action-taking Part. The goal here is to find the easiest way for you to do the right thing.

Step 5:   **Think of all of your options for action to carry out the answer you received from Step 4 above.**

If your light bulb did light, your heart knows personnel will be harmed.

Your options might be similar to the following:

1. Don't allow the tests.

2. Fully explain the tests, their possible effects and let personnel choose to participate or not.

3. Encourage the re-deployment of those engaged in development and testing of CB/W.

Step 6:   **Run each option through your mind as you visualize your light bulb. Observe the reaction of your tool. If you get a definitive, high quality light, go on to Step 7. If you don't get a high quality, definitive answer, give yourself more time to come up with additional options (Step 5) and take them back through Step 6.**

Step 7:   **Move on your right action. Remember that it's *your* answer. Do it!**

You will also *feel* this answer is right.

CHAPTER 25:
Use of Land Mines

IP If we can agree that weapons should not have (1) long-term, (2) uncontrollable, (3) catastrophic effects, (4) in an unpredictable fashion long after the conflict has passed, then land mines would not be in use. Even so, 124 nations have agreed that these weapons are inappropriate for modern warfare.

Part 1: Knowing the right thing to do or not to do

The first thing one has to do in the practice of integrity is know the right thing to do or not to do. There are four steps in this part of the process:

Step 1: **Sit quietly. Take a few deep abdominal breaths. Drop the shoulders; loosen the jaw; relax.**

Step 2: **Form your question(s) about what is right.**

Your questions might be similar to these:

1. Should the Ottawa Treaty be signed?

2. Is the maiming of citizens worldwide, for the foreseeable future, justified?

Step 3: **Visualize a big light bulb.** If the bulb lights, the answer to your question is "Yes."

Step 4: While visualizing the light bulb, ask each of the questions you formed at Step 2 and wait for your tool to give you your answer. You will also *feel* that the answer is right.

Part II. How to do the right thing

There are three steps in this *second* part of the process for practicing integrity. This is the action-taking Part. The goal here is to find the easiest way for you to do the right thing.

Step 5: Think of all of your options for action to carry out the answer you received from Step 4 above.

For the sake of this subject, let us assume your light bulb lit at the first question and remained dead at the second question of justification for impacts of land mine usage. You now "know" at a deep level that the Treaty should be signed. How can you do that and maintain the military advantage where you need it?

Your options might be like the following:

1. Announce to the members of the military-industrial establishment that the United States of America is going to eliminate the use of land mines in one year. Ask them to come up with options for achieving a similar military advantage without the long-term, unpredictable, catastrophic, uncontrollable impacts of land mines.

2. Indicate an intention to sign the Ottawa Treaty and offer rewards to industrial-military complex members for weapons designs that *do not* violate the Ottawa Treaty and its intention.

3. Sign the Treaty and begin the process of converting production efforts of the industrial-military complex toward land mines to detection and destruction efforts of the millions already laid.

Step 6: Run each option through your mind as you visualize your light bulb. Observe the reaction of your tool. If you get a definitive, bright light, go on to Step 7. If you don't get a high quality, definitive answer, give yourself more time to come up with additional options (Step 5) and take them back through Step 6.

Step 7:   **Move on your right action. Remember that it's *your* answer. Do it!**

You will also *feel* this answer is right.

CHAPTER 26:
Over-Zealous Disciplinary Action, Harassment and Scapegoating

IP If we accept the concept that commanding officers are responsible for the safety of those in their charge, then the expectation is that no harm (injury, disability or death) will come to a subordinate or recruit as a result of disciplinary action or the pranks, prejudice, or scapegoating by others in the military.

Part 1: Knowing the right thing to do or not to do

The first thing one has to do in the practice of integrity is know the right thing to do or not to do. There are four steps in this part of the process:

Step 1: **Sit quietly. Take a few deep abdominal breaths. Drop the shoulders; loosen the jaw; relax.**

Step 2: **Form your question(s) about what is right.**

A commander might ask:

1. Is this situation likely to lead to bodily harm? Mental abuse?

2. Will this action compromise the comfort of or ability to serve by the target of the action?

Step 3:   **Visualize a traffic light**. Assign green to represent "Yes;" red is a definite "NO!"

Step 4:   **While visualizing the traffic light, ask each of the questions you formed at Step 2 and wait for your tool to give you your answer. You will also *feel* that the answer is right.**

Part II. How to do the right thing

There are three steps in this *second* part of the process for practicing integrity. This is the action-taking Part. The goal here is to find the easiest way for you to do the right thing.

Step 5:   **Think of all of your options for action to carry out the answer you received from Step 4 above.**

If your traffic light is showing green, then you know you have an explosive and potentially dangerous situation. Trust your intuition. You are looking for options that might defuse the situation.

Your list might include:

1. Organize and assign those ready to cause harm to a work detail.

2. Let all subordinates know they will face court martial if they mistreat a peer or a subordinate or if harm comes to someone under their charge.

3. Follow up immediately on rumors of scapegoating or prejudicial behavior.

4. Make known to all that areas or locations historically used for clandestine rituals are off limits and that severe punishment awaits those who violate the rule.

Step 6:   **Run each option through your mind as you visualize your traffic light. Observe the reaction of your tool. If**

you get a definitive, high quality green light, go on to Step 7. If you don't get a high quality, definitive answer, give yourself more time to come up with additional options (Step 5) and take them back through Step 6.

Step 7:   Move on your right action. Remember that it's *your* answer. Do it!

You will also *feel* this answer is right.

SECTION III:

Measuring Change
In Integrity Levels

CHAPTER 27:
Using the Integrity Quotient To Measure Our Integrity Level

What is an acceptable level of integrity for an individual to have? I say we should aim for total integrity. That is, in *every* choice for action that we confront in *all* aspects of our lives *every day*, we should try to make that choice from a position of integrity. That's perfection. Most of us would assume that perfection is unattainable. Others would shudder at the possibility of being that good. It doesn't fit their self image. I have always challenged myself and others to aim high. If you aim high and don't succeed you will probably end up a lot higher than if you aimed low and *did* succeed As with any change, start slowly or gradually.

1. Either pick one relationship (e.g., your spouse, your child, your mother, your co-worker, your military commander) or a certain time of day (e.g., your lunch hour, evenings with your family, all day Saturday).

2. Consciously try to take yourself through the 7-Step Process for the Practice of Integrity whenever you face a decision — big or small.

3. After your time period is over or a period of interface with your challenge individual passes, score yourself using **The Integrity Quotient (TIQ)**. **The Integrity Quotient** is computed by dividing the *number of decisions* in which you used the 7-Step Process for Practicing Integrity *before* you acted by the number of decisions you faced. That is:

$$\frac{\text{No. of Decisions Made Using the 7-Step Process}}{\text{No. of Decisions Faced}} = \text{TIQ}$$

4. The goal is to have an **Integrity Quotient** of 1.

Remember that the 7-Step Process comes quickly with practice. That is, you will not always have to stop and visualize a tool. It is a feeling in the body that will be your indicator ... the same feeling you learned to associate with actions of your tools. At other times, Part I, knowing what is right, is instantaneous and the "how" is the problem. In such cases, you may want to check yourself by passing what you know to be right by your tool quickly and going on to Step 5 where you move slowly through Part II of the Process. In difficult cases, or where much is at stake, you are encouraged to return to the 7-Step Process. It gives you some assurance that you are not missing some options or acting too quickly.

You will be most successful if you take one challenge individual or situation at a time or try to use the 7-Step Process for longer and longer periods of time. Start with 1 hour each day and gradually increase the time you will consciously practice using the 7-Step Process. Increase the time only when you are pleased with your "performance" in the current period. You may find other approaches to using the Integrity Quotient which work better for you.

I encourage you to talk to family members, friends, and others you consider to be practicing integrity successfully. Explore their approaches to choosing the right action when they are challenged. You will be starting the conversation about integrity that will raise awareness and foster the pursuit of integrity— globally!

Believe in yourself and your ability to change. It is never too late. Human beings are among the most resilient and flexible of all creatures on the planet. Corporations and governments change directions and policies all the time. If they can, individuals certainly can.

Congratulations! You are on your way. You are sure to receive major blessings in the new millennium because of your personal efforts to improve your life and life on planet Earth.

CHAPTER 28:
Using the Integrity Quotient to Measure Integrity Levels of Political Leaders

We, the world public, have a major opportunity in the early years of the 21st century. The technology exists for us to monitor on a daily basis the actions of those we elect and support with our energy. There are websites that allow you to check on the voting decisions, latest speeches and other actions taken by our political and military leaders and the appointed officials who speak for us and represent us in international bodies. We can know immediately if a political figure has voted as he or she promised they would, has supported measures we elected them to support, has dealt away our interest or compromised the future of our planet.

The introduction of the Integrity Quotient is perfectly timed with this explosion of technology. Using both the technology and the Integrity Quotient to hold our leaders accountable we, the world public, become a formidable force. An e-mail message broadcast to others, to the officials whose actions lack integrity (and certainly to those in integrity) takes just a few minutes. We can let our leaders know we are measuring their actions against their promises. We can let appointed officials know we are a one person campaign for or against their actions. Each of us, individually — without a single postage stamp or large meeting — acting collectively can reverse the downward spiral of humanity.

To use the Integrity Quotient to measure the integrity of political officials, take the following steps:

1. Identify those individuals over whom you have some control (that is, you vote for them, they are appointed and live in your area, or they are nationally appointed or elected figures).

2. Make a written or mental list of the promises made by the individuals you have identified in Step 1 above.

3. Watch the actions of those identified above by paying attention to the newspaper, the TV or radio news, or online/Internet resources and use **The Integrity Quotient (TIQ)** equation below. Score the officials yourself using the TIQ by dividing the number of decisions they made in alignment with the promises they made by the number of opportunities to vote in alignment with the promises they made. That is:

$$\frac{\textbf{No. of Times Voted in Alignment with Promises}}{\textbf{No. of Opportunities to Vote in Alignment with Promises}} = \textbf{TIQ}$$

A specific example is:

Representative X voted to support child health 3 times

Representative X had 7 opportunities to support child health

By dividing the number of appropriate votes cast (3) by the total number of voting opportunities on that subject (7), you will arrive at the following computation:

$$\frac{3}{7} = 0.43$$

4. The goal is to have an **Integrity Quotient** of 1.

Representative X does not stand up well from an integrity stand point with a score of less than .5 (50%). This representative needs to know (s)he has a low level of integrity and that you intend to respond appropriately at the next election, will send this same information to appointing officials and/or use the information wherever and however you deem it appropriate. A few e-mails, letters or calls like this and things will begin to change. Using this method empowers us to change our world.

I encourage you to practice integrity. I encourage you to insist that those who work for us in government do the same. The 21st century can be an exciting time. It will be tumultuous with change. You can be on the right side of change by getting on board now and assisting that change to come about. Changing the downward spiral of the world is up to *you* and *me*. We've got a lot of work to do. Let's get going!

AFTERWORD

Well, now you have finished reading my thoughts on integrity. So, what have I tried to convey? First and foremost is the fact that there is an integrity crisis of global proportions. Secondly, I hope I have conveyed that we can change the current integrity deficit. That is, we can have a world where integrity is the norm in personal, local, national and international affairs. I have also laid the responsibility for this at our feet. This change can only happen with our conscious decision to make it happen.

Our world is changing faster than at any other time in human history. We, the world community, have generated the energy which is propelling us at this unprecedented rate. I have challenged us, the world community, to harness some of this same energy and direct it in ways that grow the level of integrity right along with the growth in our economies and our personal assets. We *can* have it all.

What I have also said is that the *power* to change — your "voice of integrity" is within you. I am just the messenger. What I have tried to stress is that the *power* — the voice — is not something you have to get. You already have it. It is something to access. Much of this volume has focused on one technique for accessing your power — your own voice of integrity.

I have also suggested that our ways have been driven by our fears. The best way for us to enhance our sense of security in this new century is to start thinking globally and acting locally. In other words, by practicing integrity as I've described here — in our own personal lives, on our jobs, in our towns and on our streets, in our town halls and legislative houses — our actions come into alignment with a new global reality. By giving up the self-defeating behavior of the past and embracing a different way to be in the world, we create relationships built on our mutual goals. We all want the same things, you know. The potential is awesome!

In the last two decades of the 20th century, there were several examples of people's unwillingness to continue to experience harsh limitations on the human spirit. In Europe we witnessed the toppling of the Berlin Wall in defiance of the old world order. We saw the Union of Soviet Socialist Republics fall in three days when citizens withdrew their support. We have seen officials with the mandate of the people in some of our island nations, define the socio-economic structure they felt would best meet the needs of their citizens and assert their right to pursue them. We saw examples of it in Jamaica under the leadership of Michael Manley, again in Grenada with Maurice Bishop and in Cuba with Fidel Castro. Some have prevailed against external pressure, others have not. In the same two decades, we have seen Eastern, Middle Eastern and African powers defy those who would control the world order; some have prevailed.

The coming decades will bring more movement in this direction. What I hope I have conveyed is that in the next decades one group will not be able to hold the world back and force it to have it's relationships dictated. And that's not a bad thing. One group should not be able to prevent the evolution of the human spirit wherever it manifests itself in the world . That force, which is in all of us, will express itself in a multiplicity of ways all over the globe. We must not fear it. We must embrace it. The practice of integrity requires us to look for the best options for all in any situation. It gives us a way to embrace change.

So, have you dared to dream about the possibilities in a world where integrity is the foundation of all human interaction? No? Well, if you try, you will feel a smile spread across your face. If you would allow yourself to even contemplate the magnificence of such a world, it would lift your spirits.

Go ahead. Think about it. Close your eyes and visualize it. Your children would feel respected and cared for but would be clear about their limits and the consequences of exceeding them. Your loved ones would feel respected and accepted for what they are and would feel you wanted them to find their highest good. Co-workers would feel appreciated and respected and that they and their colleagues were being fairly judged and compensated within the agency's capacity to compensate them. The boss would feel he got a full day's work from his employees. Friends and lovers would feel honored instead of used; they would know where they stood and could drop their defenses and leave the games behind. Teachers could give children the comfort they often need without fear of a lawsuit. People of different religions, races and cultural groups - everywhere in the world, could walk the streets and byways without fearing for their lives. The conflicts would be settled using the intelligence of men and women rather than through their emotions made more dangerous by weapons.

I don't want to sound naive or unrealistic. Practicing integrity prepares the way for everything else. It is not all we have to do to solve the world's problems. But all else will fail if not built on a foundation of integrity – doing the best thing for the greater good.

If we could achieve the personal and interpersonal ease suggested above, by logical extension, there would be no fear of bombing attacks because disagreements would be settled without violence. There would be no famine, no hungry children with vacant eyes staring into the cameras because those who have an abundance of food would make sure that those without food can still eat. They would realize that what they did with excess food required the practice of integrity for the global good. Devastating diseases would not decimate whole cultures because others who have protective vaccines and medicines would assure these were made available; they would know that what affects one affects us all. Water resources would be pure and clean because we would recognize the cyclical nature of our use of natural resources and we would use them in a way that is best for the global good. The elderly, the working poor and those unable to earn their way would have health care and their needs would be met. We could do these things because the will would be there and the wastes of financial resources would have been eliminated.

Go ahead. Think about it. What do you see? Remember, thoughts are things. If you can imagine it, you can create it. If you can dream it, you can manifest it. Dare to create a magnificent future for us all!

I hope you have enjoyed reading this book. If you did, please recommend it to others. I also hope you will engage others in conversations about integrity. Share the skills you have learned from reading this book and encourage others to practice integrity. But most of all, I hope you will practice integrity yourself and be the beacon — the kind of leader that others can follow toward a global society.

Please write me and share your experiences using the 7-Step Process for Practicing Integrity. Tell me about your successes. Tell me what you had trouble with or what was difficult. In that way our future work can address some of your challenges and others may benefit from your efforts.

Gwen Smith Brown
c/o Soul Source Press, Inc.
P.O. Box 590
Temple Hills, MD 20748-0590

NOTES

1.   Daniel Schorr originally delivered the foreword as the Keynote Address at The 1999 Forum on Citizenship at the John F. Kennedy Library & Museum, October 4, 1999. It is used here with his permission, for which I am deeply grateful.

2.   A very brief report on this survey appeared in the June 19 - 21, 1998 issue of *USA Today* under the feature heading "USA Snapshots." "Always tell the truth" was the most frequent (33%) response adults gave regarding the most important thing they learned from their father.

3.   The French government transfused hundreds of its citizens with unscreened blood at a time when Human Immunodeficiency Virus (HIV) was known to be blood-borne and believed to cause Acquired Immune Deficiency Syndrome (AIDS). Over 400 individuals who received these transfusions have died. Many law suits have been filed by victims and their families. The reports on the trials discussed here appeared on March 10, 1999 in Associated Press and Reuters Limited articles retrieved via the Internet.

4.   Statistics on extra-marital affairs are taken from "The Monogamy Myth and the Prevalence of Affairs" by Peggy Vaughan, available at website http://www.vaughan-vaughan.com/statistics.html. Ms. Vaughan has looked at a wide range of studies on the subject of monogamy in marriage. She says that most people believe in and want [monogamy] for themselves and that most surveys bear this out. In fact, in surveys, most people feel monogamy is important to marriage and that affairs are wrong. Similarly, most people intend to be monogamous when they get married. Not withstanding the belief in monogamy, in 1989 the general consensus of researchers who have studied the issue was that more than 25% and possibly as many as 50% of women and 50% to

65% of men have had lovers while married. With the changes in society — including the number of women having affairs on the Internet and the increased number of women in the workforce— the estimate is that by 1998, the percentage of married women having affairs is 60% which is similar to the percentage of men who have been involved in extra-marital relationships. That number is believed to be essentially unchanged at 65%.

5. *Practice of integrity* is a term being introduced in this work. I coined the phrase to describe the 2-part process required to (a) know what is right; and (b) select from among the options for doing the right thing that option which is most comfortable for you. For more extensive discussion of the term, see Chapter 1.

6. The meaning of integrity is taken from *Webster's Encyclopedic Unabridged Dictionary of the English Language,* published by Portland House, NY, 1989. This is the reference used for definitions of all subsequent terms unless otherwise stated.

7. Dr. Wayne W. Dyer, well known author and lecturer whose books include *Real Magic* and best seller *Your Erroneous Zones,* talks about his practice of gratefulness on his audio tape program, "The Secrets to Manifesting Your Destiny" which is a Nightingale-Conant product.

8. M. Scott Peck, M.D. *The Road Less Traveled*, New York: Simon & Schuster, 1978.

9. Homily delivered by Fr. Richard A. Scott at St. John The Evangelist Roman Catholic Church, Clinton, MD, September 14, 1998.

10. President Bill Clinton gave the keynote address to the United Nations General Assembly on September 22, 1998. His topic was terrorism. As he came on stage to take his seat near the lectern, delegates rose and started a standing ovation. He was later embraced by Mr. Nelson Mandela.

11.   There was an extensive assessment of the possible long term
      impact of the Monica Lewinsky affair on the institution of
      the presidency and the pervasiveness of the damage on insti-
      tutions of government in "A Year of Scandal With No
      Winners" which appeared in *The Washington Post* on
      February 11, 1999, p. A1.

12.   The viciousness of the 1998 campaigns is exemplified in the
      following cases which are cited for their extreme nature:

      A. Byron "Low Tax" Looper was Putnam County,
          Tennessee's property assessor running against the pop-
          ular incumbent, state Senator Tommy Burks, for his
          Senate seat. Looper was arrested on October 23, 1998,
          arraigned and charged with the murder of Tommy Burks
          who was shot as he sat in his truck several days earlier.

      B. In the race for the Senate in New York, Democratic
          Congressman Charles E. Schumer called incumbent
          Senator Alfonse D'Amato "Senator Pothole." The two
          went toe-to-toe in televison attacks producing a frantic
          and frequently ugly race in which New Yorkers were
          subjected to two months of commercials so ugly that the
          later polls showed they had soured the stomachs of
          many voters and raised the negative feelings they had for
          both candidates. D'Amato's greatest weakness going
          into the campaign was reported to be the strong negative
          reaction to his name evoked among 60% of New York
          voters for their "perceptions of the Senator's ethics prob-
          lems" including the wide-spread belief that his legisla-
          tive muscle could be purchased with large campaign
          contributions. He attacked his opponent (Schumer) with
          statements like, "a liberal from Brooklyn" (i.e., a Jew) and
          "a putzhead" (Yiddish slur literally meaning penis head
          and often softened to "fool.")

      C. In South Carolina, Republican governor David M.
          Beasley was defeated by Democrat Jim Hodges. Beaslely
          accused the Democrats of spreading a false rumor about
          him having an extra-marital affair.

      D. Also in South Carolina, Republican Representative Bob
          Inglis conducted a self-proclaimed "courteous cam-

paign" against incumbent Senator Ernest Hollings who retained his seat with 53% of the vote. Hollings called Inglis, who also turned down money from PACs (political action committees), "a god damn skunk" and derided what he called "self-righteousness."

E. In Georgia, incumbent governor Zell Miller was defeated by Democratic challenger Roy Barnes. Barnes faced a barrage of ugly late campaign ads attacking him for supporting affirmative action.

Additionally, campaigns in California, Arizona, Michigan and New Mexico all made the news for their viciousness. (These specifics are from *The Washington Post*, October 24, 1998 and November 4, 1998.)

13. 1998 Information Please Almanac, Boston: Information Please, LLC. 1997, pg. 65, Table: National Voter Turnout in Federal Elections: 1960-1996 and *The Washington Post*, November 5, 1998, pg. A33. The pattern of voter participation which emerges from study of the Table is that the percentage of eligible voters who exercise their privilege to vote has been dropping since 1960. The 1960 rate was 63.1%; in 1996, only 49.1% of those eligible to vote actually did. Off-year (non-presidential) elections typically have 13% to 17% less voter turnout. Over the last 30 years, that percentage has dropped from a high of 48.4% in 1966 to a low of 36.4% in 1986. The 1998 off-year turnout was reported at 36% and 38% in the electronic press.

14. Analysis of the final FY '99 budget appeared in *The Washington Post* on October 21, 1998, Section A, p1, col 3. This and two other articles on October 20, 1998, Section A, p3, col 1 and 4 gave specifics on the individual Members' pet projects included in the budget.

15. T.R. Martin ("Ethics in Marketing: Problems and Prospects") published in *Marketing Ethics: Guidelines for Managers*, Gene R. Laczniak & Patrick E. Murphy, Lexington Books, Lexington, MA, 1986. Pg. 4) cites the example of the significant fall in highway building costs in the 1980's. The costs dropped after federal Department of Transportation investi-

gations of and prosecutions for bid-rigging, which began in 1979. Exposure of the price- fixing schemes led to at least 180 companies and 200 executives being fined and/or jailed.

16.   A discussion of the C-130s can be found in The Washington Post of June 25, 1998, pg. A6 in an article entitled, "Aircraft Spending Priorities Draw Rebukes." Also, in a Washington Post article on July 23, 1998 (Section A, pg. 17: The Federal Page, "Cargo Plane With Strings Attached: Congress Funds and Stations C-130s Unwanted by Pentagon") the action of the Appropriations Committee, lobbied by Gingrich, and of the full Congress on that aspect of the 1999 budget is reported. Network news reports during the summer of 1998 indicated that the then-Speaker also sent a letter to the Pentagon suggesting they request eight (8) C-130Js in 2000 and twelve (12) C-130Js each year thereafter.

17.   Toure Mohammad's article, "Controversial African trade bill still draws mixed reviews from African officials, Blacks" in *Final Call,* July 21, 1998, describes the Africa Growth Opportunity Act proposed by President Bill Clinton. At the time of this article, the bill was going to the Senate for a vote. This new trade agreement is supposed to lower tariffs and make export requirements less stringent thereby making it easier for Africans to have access to our market and Americans to have access to Africa's markets. Critics argue that the bill has unfavorable provisions for African countries. University of Maryland Political Science professor, Ron Walters, points to the International Monetary Fund and World Bank requirements of the bill and other provisions which compromise African countries' sovereignty.

18.   Students on campuses throughout California have demonstrated from the beginning against the efforts of the Regents to dismantle affirmative action in admissions. Even those denied admission feel it is important to have a multi-ethnic/multi-racial environment on campuses. Students have long argued that their education is enhanced by the presence of a multi-cultural student body. A new study appears to have proven them right — albeit too late to help University of California students in their fight to save affirmative action.

The study is discussed in William Raspberry's column (*The Washington Post*, October 2, 1998, pg. A27) It appears that two eminent educators, William Bowen, former president of Princeton University, and Derek Bok, former president of Harvard University have analyzed databases, built by the Andrew W. Mellon Foundation, on three cohorts of students at 28 elite universities. Their conclusion is that by virtually any reasonable measure, affirmative action works — exactly as the students assert. In addition, the overall success rate of black students is 75% compared to 85% for white students a difference which is too small to support critics assertions that black students admitted via affirmative action programs are less capable. For the complete discussion of the data, see Bowen and Bok's *The Shape of the River: Long-Term Consequences of Considering Race in College and University Admissions*, Princeton University Press, 1998.

19.   For a thorough account of the California struggle over affirmative action in university admissions and the ensuing effort to eliminate affirmative action throughout the country, read *The Lynching of Affirmative Action* by Frederick E. Jordan, published by Wizard Publications, San Francisco, CA 1998.

20.   For a discussion of what is asserted to be the development of the AIDS virus, see *A Survey of Chemical and Biological Warfare*, by John Cookson and Judith Nottingham, published by Sheed and Ward, London, 1969, pp. 275-282.

21.   For a thorough discussion of this American tragedy, see *Bad Blood: The Tuskegee Syphilis Experiment*, by James H. Jones, New York: The Free Press (Macmillan), 1981. Also, the 1997 film, "Miss Eunice's Boys" chronicles the Experiment. Articles also appeared in popular publications at the time the experiment was disclosed including *Time Magazine* ("A Matter of Morality," August 7, 1972, p.54) and *Ebony Magazine* ("Condemned to Die for Science," November 1972 pp. 177+)

22.   Lobotomies and their use in prisons in California are described in *The Progressive Review*, February 9, 1972 issue, page 3 in an article, "Prison Reform California Style:

Neurosurgical Treatment for Violent Inmates" and in *Science News* ("A clockwork orange in a California prison," March 11, 1972, vol. 101, p.174-175. In the March 22, 1972 issue of *The Progressive Review*, (p. 17) there is a discussion of lobotomies in an article entitled, "Lobotomies and Psychosurgery". Additional articles explored this emerging practice including one explaining the resurgence in psychosurgery, which appeared in *Time Magazine* ("Psychosurgery Returns," April 3, 1972, p.50), and others on psychosurgery's questionable results, side effects and especially, the motives for use found in *Newsweek Magazine* ("Psychosurgery Under Fire," March 27, 1972, p.63) and *Science News* ("Debate over psychosurgery continues," March 18, 1972 ,vol. 101, p.182).

23.   The New York Times, August 30, 1997 v146 n242 p18(N) p22 (L) col 1)

24.   Statistics on land mines and their devastation are provided by May Khadem, M.D., Chicago Disaster Relief Subcommittee, American Academy of Ophthalmology, in a letter to Ann Landers which appeared in the September 11, 1998 "Ann Landers" column in *The Washington Post*, Pg E1.

25.   Citations for the incidents reported here are as follows:

   A.   *The Washington Post*, Nov 14,1996 v119 n345 pA9 col1 "Navy, Air Force to review explanation of sexual harassment policy to personnel."

   B.   *The New York Times* December 27, 1996 v146 (N) pA24 "Air Force Demotes General."

   C.   *The New York Times* February 24, 1998 v147 pA12 (N) pA14 (L) col 5 "Prosecutors Rest Case Against Sergeant Major."

26.   *The New York Times*, July 15, 1999 pA16 (L) col 4.

INDEX

60 Minutes, 36

A

Aberdeen Ordinance Center, 46
accountability, 11
Acquired Immune Deficiency Syndrome (AIDS), development, 42,
    France, xix, 123
Afghanistan, xviii
Agent Orange, 45
Air Force, sexual harassment, 46, 128
appointed officials, 29-30, 40, 116, integrity challenges, 29-41, 80-101,
    90, 99
Army, sexual harassment, 46

B

baby-boomers, 35
Berlin Wall, 23, 120
Bishop, Maurice, 120

C

C-130J cargo aircraft, 36, 127
Caribbean Basin Initiative, 37, 38
Castro, Fidel, 120
chemical weapons, testing, 42-45, 102, 104, 128
chemical and biological warfare, development, 42-45, 102, 104, 128
Chinese, 23, 34
civil servants, xxii, 64, 90, integrity challenges, 24-28, 61-79
conflict of interest, 26
Congress, United States, xviii, 15, 32-33, 36, 38, budget development, 36-37, 127, destruction of, 30, 33, 80-82, impeachment, 31
Connerly, Ward, 40-41
contributions, political, 87, 125
Cuba, 120, Cubans, 34

D

de-emphasizing the truth, 26, 70
Dyer, Wayne, 15, 124

E

elected officials, xvii, xxii, integrity challenges, 29-41, 80-101
employee recognition, system for, 28, 78
ethical behavior, 12-13
ethnic cleansing, xviii
Europe, xvii, 40, 120

F

foreign policy, 34
Fort Dietrick, 43
funding decisions, 26, 67

G

Geneva Accord, 102
Gingrich, Newt, 36, 127
global society, 38, 40, 122, significance, 4
Grenada, 120

H

honesty, xix, 3-4, 11, 13, 26
Hussein, Saddam, xviii

I

individual authority, 17-18
Inner Voice, 16, 20, 105
integrity, xvii, xix, definition, 13, global imperative, xvii,
    measurement of, xxiii, 113-115, measurement of leaders, xxii, 116-117
    practicing (See practice of integrity)
    support system for, xxi
integrity crisis, xvii, xix
integrity position, 7, definition, 49
international organizations, misuse of, 38, 96
International Monetary Fund (IMF), 38-39, 127

L

land mines, 42, 45, 106-107, 129
life purpose, 20-21, 53
lobbyists, 34, 86
lobotomies, 43, 128-129
Lockheed Martin, 36
loyalty, definition of, 12

M

Mandela, Nelson, 31, 124
Manley, Michael, 120
McKinney, Sgt. Maj. Gene C., 46
Mexico, 38
military officials, disciplinary action, 46
    integrity challenges for, 42-47, 102-111
Milosevic, Slobodan, 39

N

NAFTA (North Atlantic Free Trade Agreement), 37
Navy, sexual harassment, 46, 125
Newell, Brig. Gen. Robert T., 46
North Korea, xvii
North Atlantic Treaty Organization (NATO), 39

O

old world order, 120
oneself, 16, 19-20, 58
Ottawa Treaty, 45, 106-107

P

partisanship, 30, 32-33, 84

Peck, M. Scott, 19, 124

Pentagon, 36-37, 127

personal integrity, challenges to, 14-23, 51-60

political action committees (PACs), 34, 126

pork, 36, barrels, 30, 34, 36, 90-91

power, your own, 11, 19-20, 51, 119

power to change, 119

practice of integrity, xix-xxiii, 12, 15, 27, 49, 51, 53, 55, 58, 61, 64, 67, 70,
     72, 76, 80, 84, 87, 90, 93, 97, 99, 102, 104, 106, 109, 113, 120, 124
     definition, 4
     7-Step Process for the, 9
     tools for the, 8

prejudice, 22-23, 50, 59, 108

presidency, destruction of, 30-31, 81-82, 125

President Bill Clinton, xiv, xviii, 31, 40, 124, 127

public funds, misuse by employees, 25

R

racism, 22, 28, 58

Russia, xviii

Rwanda, xviii

S

scapegoating, 42, 46, 109-110

Self, 5, 16-17, 19

selling the vote, 30, 34, 87

sexism, 22, 28, 58

sexual harassment, xviii, 24, 46, 61, 129, definition, 24

Social Security investment fund, 35

special interest groups (SIGs), 34

Special Counsel investigations, Starr, 31

sterilizations, unrequested, 43

students, cheating, xix

Sudan, xviii

T

The Integrity Quotient (TIQ), xxiii, 113-117
tools (See practice of integrity)
trade agreements, 30, 37, 93
treaties, lopsided, 30, 36, 93
Turkey, xviii
Tuskegee Syphilis Experiment, 43, 128

U

United Nations, xviii, 31, 38-40, 124
Union of Soviet Socialist Republics, 23, 120

V

Victory at Sea, 44
Voice of Integrity, 19, 119 (Also see Inner Voice)
voter turnout, xiv, 126

W

Walters, Ph.D., Ronald, 38, 127
wasting money, 30 ,34, 90
weapons of mass destruction, xvii-xviii, 136
whistle blower, 73, definition, 27
Wilson, Pete, 40
Winchell, Barry, 47
World Bank, 38-39, 127

Y

Yugoslavia, xviii, 39

DISCLAIMERS

This book is designed to provide information on achieving a global society that functions with integrity. It is sold with the understanding that the reader seeks a general understanding of one process which can bring about that integrity. However, neither the author nor the publisher claim to be professional counselors or divine interventionists. For difficult, health threatening and/or life-threatening matters, the reader is advised to seek assistance from the appropriate professional trained to handle such matters. Similarly, the author and publisher take no responsibility for world events of a minor or major nature. Further, the author and publisher take no responsibility for events and changes in the lives and personal situations of readers who practice integrity.

Readers are encouraged to carefully consider the personal risks involved and practice the method described herein if and only if they are prepared to accept full responsibility for any and all outcomes.

The Author
LaVOIX, Inc.
Soul Source Press, Inc.

ABOUT THE AUTHOR

GWEN SMITH BROWN's first book, *The Integrity Manual for Leaders in a Global Society*, marks her entry into her fourth career — that of author, speaker and publisher.   As the voice of Jane Q. Public, Brown verbalizes the most basic longing of the average citizens of the world: that is, the desire for personal integrity, integrity in their children, the people with whom they do business and those among whom they live, work and play. Brown's 7-Step Process for Practicing Integrity has been hailed as "..so simple it's profound." It is so simple that children use the process with ease. Two additional Integrity Manuals will be published over the coming months: *The Integrity Manual for Individuals in a Global Society* and *The Integrity Manual for Ministers, Managers, and Moguls in a Global Society.* Each is written for the general public in Brown's simple, straightforward manner.

Brown's company is LaVOIX, Inc. La VOIX is French for "the Voice." The company will assist individuals, organizations, corporations and governments to bring integrity into their lives and work through presentations, workshops, management training and mediation. LaVOIX is also engaged in the creation of multimedia products and other services that support the global practice of integrity.

Brown is an engaging speaker, powerful workshop presenter and accomplished trainer. She has presented at numerous national meetings and conferences and planned and facilitated workshops for large and small groups. Brown's earlier careers included civil service with the United States government, program development and funding with a large national health foundation and management consulting with corporate and non-profit organizations in the San Francisco Bay Area.

WHAT IS LaVOIX, INC.?

LaVOIX (pronounced "la VWA") is French for "the Voice." It is based in the Washington, D.C. suburb of Temple Hills, Maryland, USA.

WHAT SERVICES ARE OFFERED BY LaVOIX, INC.?

We at LaVOIX are dedicated to:

1. assisting individuals, organizations, companies and governments to understand how to bring integrity into their personal lives, their work and their societies;

2. promoting and encouraging dialog about the struggle for integrity as well as its winning moments; and

3. providing services marked by integrity to support the progress of our global society. Services include:

- Speeches
- Management training
- Books on integrity
- Workshops
- Mediation

To arrange any of these services, for additional information, to obtain a schedule of appearances by Gwen Smith Brown, or to be placed on our mailing list, please contact us at:

LaVOIX, Inc.
P.O. Box 590
Temple Hills, MD 20748-0590
E-mail: LaVoixInc@aol.com
Phone: 301-505-8109 Fax: 301-505-7017

Order Form

Quantity	Title	Unit Cost	Total Cost
	The Integrity Manual for Leaders in		
_____	**A Global Society** — by G. S. Brown	$_____	$_____

Tax: *(for books shipped to Maryland addresses)* @ 5% $_____

Shipping/Postage: *(See Below)* $_____

Handling Charges: $____1.50____

Total Included $_____

Order On-line: Visit the publisher's website: **SoulSourcePress.com**

Postal Orders: Send copy of this form with money orders or checks to: Soul Source Press, Inc, P.O. Box 590, Temple Hills, MD 20748-0590

Fax Orders: 301-505-7017

Ship to: Name _____

Address _____

_____

May we add you to our mailing list? _____Yes _____No

Contact publisher (301-505-8109) for rates not shown below:

SHIPPING COSTS

No. of Books Ordered

Shipping	1	2-3	4-6	7-8
1st Class USPS	$2.30	3.20	5.40	6.50
Book Rate USPS	1.13	1.58	2.03	2.48

MULTIPLE BOOK DISCOUNTS

No. of Books Ordered

Shipping	1-3	4-9	10-24	25-199	200-399	400+
Cost per Book	17.95	12.55	11.67	10.77	9.87	8.98
% Discount	0	30	35	40	45	50